P9-BHY-656

# The IQ Cult

also by the author

A PARENT'S GUIDE TO THE NEW MATHEMATICS

A PARENT'S GUIDE TO MORE NEW MATH

NEW MATHEMATICS READER

THINKING IS CHILD'S PLAY

# The IQ Cult

EVELYN SHARP

Coward, McCann & Geoghegan
New York

# *Contents*

# Part I
# The Path We Have Traveled

# Chapter I
## From Awe to Anathema

*"It is pretty shocking to know that a local business man, just by saying he's considering hiring your daughter, can get more information from the schools about her capabilities . . . than you could get during all the years she was growing up."*

*This remark, reported in the New York* Times *in February, 1961, summed up the parents' side of a fiery disagreement over whether they had the right to see their children's school records, including IQ scores. The New York State Education Department ruled that they did, but some schools were reluctant to break the long-standing tradition that such data are sacrosanct and not for parents' eyes.*

*When a junior high school in East Meadow, Long Island, refused Edward Van Allen's request to inspect his son's records, he took his case to the State Supreme Court and won.* (Van Allen vs. McCleary.)

---

*In March, 1964, the New York City Board of Education announced that, starting with the following fall, the city's public schools would do away with group IQ tests. Dr. Joseph Loretan, deputy superintendent for research*

11

*and evaluation, said in a directive sent to 800 school principals that group IQ tests "can present a misleading picture of a student's abilities." He added, "The fact that a child obtains a low score on a group IQ test does not necessarily mean that he is incapable of learning, nor does a high score on a group IQ test necessarily mean that the child will not encounter difficulties in certain aspects of the curriculum."*

*Some other large cities, including Washington and Los Angeles, also discontinued group IQ testing in public schools.*

---

*The U.S. Supreme Court, in the Duke Power Company case, declared unlawful the company's practice of making an IQ test part of the requirement for promotion to the job of coal handler at their Dan River, North Carolina, plant. In a unanimous decision handed down in March, 1971, the justices ruled that any test given must relate directly to the skills needed on the job in question.*

---

*A federal court in Philadelphia ordered Pennsylvania to assure an education for all mentally retarded children in the state, starting in September, 1972. In Pennsylvania, as elsewhere, retarded children are customarily divided into three categories according to IQ score. Ranging downward, these are the educable mentally retarded, the trainable mentally retarded, and the uneducable and untrainable. Once a child is placed in that third, dead-end category, the schools are relieved of their obligation to train him, and it was this group in whose behalf the suit was brought (and won).*

*Pennsylvania Governor Milton Shapp praised the decision and was quoted in* Time *as saying that it "recognized the relative ineffectiveness of IQ tests as a gauge of the development potential of a retarded child."*

---

There are only two periods in the history of any strongly entrenched cult when its tenets are openly and critically discussed. One is when it is just coming into power; the other is when it is crumbling. That the stranglehold the IQ cult has had on the public is slipping, the news stories above plainly show. Therefore it's not surprising to find some of the same questions being hotly debated today that were hotly debated fifty years ago.

For one, IQ tests test something, all right, but is it what they say it is? What constitutes intelligence? I asked a school psychologist, and she said, "You mean what it is that we're measuring?" She hesitated a little. "There have been so many theories of intelligence, all different. Nobody really knows. I don't like to talk about it."

Another is the old controversy of nature versus nurture. Is intelligence determined more by heredity or by environment? This is a flesh-and-blood question—a gut issue that touches the lives of millions. Because if intelligence is chiefly in the genes—a position that has recently been put forward again—then efforts to improve people's environment won't do much good.

But the data that these new hereditarians are basing their arguments on are the comparative scores made by different groups and races on the same old IQ tests. If these are to be our gauges, we'd better scrutinize them closely before making any decisions derived from their readings.

Precisely because the IQ tests are no longer considered sacred, it is now possible to look at them out in the open, where what they are becomes a little plainer. Our present tests come from a common stock. They are either descendants or mutations of an examination that Alfred Binet developed for the Parisian school system in the early 1900's to identify who could, and who could not, do the schoolwork *as the schools were then*. Based on no theory of intelligence, they were simply meant to sort children out. Furthermore, he never said that his test was independent of the amount of opportunity that a child had had to learn some of the things called for in the tests. That idea is part of the IQ cult that grew up in this country.

The Binet test that we adopted was only a small part out of the whole of his work in differential psychology. Some of his tests were ridiculous; some showed promise. He died at the age of fifty-four without having time to pursue very far the possibilities that his experiments opened up. Of all those tests that appeared promising, we froze onto one alone, because it correlated with the schoolwork of the time. Perhaps we were too hasty in overlooking the rest.

Other streams from the Binet wellspring have gone in different directions. When Swiss psychologist Jean Piaget worked at the Binet laboratory as a young man, he became interested in investigating what lay behind children's wrong answers rather than merely tabulating their right ones. From that beginning, he has spent a lifetime studying the way a child perceives the world and grasps ideas and deals with problems at different stages from infancy on. He has uncovered a series of signs of mental growth, each showing that a child has achieved one more step along the path to reasoning. And Piaget does not argue that the child who reaches a certain point quicker is necessarily the smarter. What matters more is how far he is going.

Although Piaget himself was not interested in constructing an instrument for measurement, there are currently underway experiments by others aimed at preparing a scale of mental development based on Piaget's work—notably those of Adrien Pinard at the University of Montreal, who would do away with the IQ type of evaluation. (See Chapter 7.) As criticism of traditional tests is mounting, these and other new approaches are coming into prominence.

Erosion of faith in the IQ cult took place gradually, little by little. The order of the progressive steps by which disenchantment set in is noteworthy.

First—and rightly so—came the attack on secrecy, so necessary to a cult. Very important values in American society imply that it is a basic right of individuals to know what information about themselves is made available to others. Yet a pupil's IQ score is put on his permanent record to follow him through school and beyond, when he applies for admission to college or for a job, but all too often neither he nor his parents are permitted to see it.

What they get is an "interpretation" by a counselor, teacher, or principal. This interpretation may be skillful and accurate, or it may be faulty and misleading, depending on the counselor's qualifications in the psychometric field, and these range from excellent to nil. (It is usually only the problem children who are referred to the school psychologist—that is, if the school has one at all. The chances of a typical pupil's being tested by a specialist are slight.)

In any case, what the parents get is secondhand. In many places, the situation still parallels that formerly enjoyed by the credit bureaus when they could supply information to banks, stores, insurance companies, and employers without the subject's knowledge. In the Fair Credit Reporting Act of April, 1971, Congress spelled out an individual's right to examine the bureau's files if he is rejected for a loan, job, or insurance policy because of an unfavorable credit report. School records constitute an even more awesome and unregulated information network that affects millions.

Secrecy of scores was only part of the whole IQ mystique that at one time held the entire test-making process to be beyond the public ken and above criticism. Back in the 1930's, when Oscar Buros—the Ralph Nader of testing and a man ahead of his time—proposed a consumer research organization that would be a sort of

bureau of standards to test the tests, there were cries of
outrage.

Because of lack of funds he didn't succeed in setting up
his bureau, but he started publishing a series of *Mental
Measurement Yearbooks*, now six in number. In these,
standardized tests (and he covered nearly everything
marketed in the English-speaking countries) are
critically reviewed, just like any other type of writing for
publication and sale— which is what tests are, of course.

Next to come under attack was the group IQ test,
admittedly a rough screening device and therefore
vulnerable. Dr. Loretan, in defending the action of the
New York City schools, made a great distinction between the group tests, which were banned, and the individually administered tests, which were kept for
specific cases, although expense, time, and personnel
requirements made them prohibitive for use with large
numbers.

In an article, "The Decline and Fall of Group Intelligence Testing" (*Teachers College Record*, October,
1965), he laid the blame for IQ evils on the mass sub-
stitution of the group test for the test given "under
controlled conditions by a specially trained psychologist
who can draw out the best in a child and who can remain
sensitive to the level of the child's motivation during
testing."

Instead of this, what the child got was the forty-five-
minute group test "usually administered to him by a
teacher untrained in testing, whose only qualification is
the ability to read the 'Directions to Teachers' on the
first page of the manual. By these means, he is identified,
labelled, [and] classified."

Many school supervisors and others objected to the
ban as a dramatic step that seemed to them too hasty.
But the Sunday New York *Times*, commenting on the
action, said that the major reason for discontinuing the
group tests appeared to be that school authorities and

educational theorists in past years tended to be deaf to criticisms of intelligence testing.

It was also the group test that was hit by the Supreme Court ruling in the Duke Power case. An article in *Business Week*, leading off with the sentence "Must a fork-lift operator know the difference between 'censor' and 'censure'?" said that the action kicked off a week of urgent consultation among personnel men, corporate lawyers, and test marketers. They added that the most immediate impact of the decision was on the standardized timed IQ test, although the industrial market for such tests is less than $5,000,000 a year, compared to the $55,000,000 educational testing market.

But it was the Philadelphia court decision that struck at the heart of the IQ stronghold—the individual test. In Pennsylvania, as in most other states, mental retardation must be determined by an individually administered examination given by a qualified psychologist.

According to information supplied by the State-Federal Information Clearinghouse for Exceptional Children, in all states there are rules and regulations that specify operating procedures for state and local education agencies. Sometimes these are written in the law; sometimes they appear in the administrative literature, such as bulletins from the department of education. "The majority of programs for the educable mentally handicapped seem to involve children whose intelligence level, on individual standardized tests, falls within the 50 to 80 [IQ] range. Programs for the trainable mentally handicapped seem usually to include children whose intelligence quotient ranges from 30 to 50. . . ."

The use of individual tests as the basis for putting children in these special education classes for the mentally retarded has been attacked before. There are two individually administered tests that dominate the field—the Stanford-Binet and the Wechsler Intelligence Scale for Children. Both were standardized on sample populations of children, all of whom were white. In the case of the Stanford-Binet, they were also all native born.

At the 1971 convention of the National Association of School Psychologists, the blacks and Mexican-Americans present made the point that the percentage of minority groups assigned to special education classes is larger than the percentage of these minority groups in the population as a whole. They felt that the IQ tests were being used to segregate them.

In fifty years, the IQ test has gone from an object of awe to an anathema in some quarters. We've tried changing the name, but the children aren't fooled. "Is this an IQ test?" they say.

There is a growing uneasiness about the effects their use will have on society as a whole. What the psychometrician does is now seen to have repercussions in the fields of sociology, economics, and politics. Because the old debate of heredity versus environment has flared up again, we can add genetics to the list.

I chose the word "psychometrician" carefully. The field of psychology, like medicine, has many specialties. Because a man is a psychologist, it doesn't necessarily follow that he is an expert on the subject of IQ tests. Let's suppose that a prominent heart surgeon, in writing an article on surgery for a popular magazine, decided to include three or four pages on obstetrics—a subject that he hadn't studied since he was in medical school or practiced since he was an intern fifteen years earlier. It would be immediately apparent that he was out of his field. Yet a prominent psychologist can write a well-publicized article, include several pages of similarly outdated material on IQ tests, and few people are aware of the fact.

The amount of misinformation and noninformation

that the public has about IQ tests is stupendous—a holdover from the days of secrecy. If you don't tell people things, they make them up.

True, the better test makers now clearly state facts in their manuals giving limitations as well as positive features. For example, "It should be clearly understood that the Otis-Lennon tests do not measure the innate mental capacity of the pupil. There is, indeed, no test of mental ability which can support such a claim." (*Manual for Administration. Otis-Lennon Mental Ability Test*, 1967, page 4.)

But how many people read manuals? Manuals are like the labels on cans—accurate, factual, and full of hard words. How many people read can labels? What prevails is advertising.

The public image of IQ testing—fostered by the solemnity and awesomeness with which early practitioners cloaked the process, handing down their findings like judgments from on high—is veiled in layers of myth, folklore, and misconception.

For instance, most people know that a score somewhere in the neighborhood of 100 is average, but average of what? The usual idea is that it is the average of the national population as a whole, or possibly all the people who took the test that year.

It is no such thing. The average is computed from the scores made by people in the sample population used to standardize the test. In all probability the sample was taken years ago, since there is a tendency to keep using the old tests. Maybe it comprised a few hundred people, maybe it included thousands.

It's as if you took a shoe from each of a number of eight-year-old children, averaged the size of all the shoes, and lined them up from smallest to largest, with the average size in the middle. Then have the whole array bronzed and for the next twenty years or so rate all shoes for eight-year-olds by comparing them with your sample. This goes for every kind of footwear—moccasins, huaraches, snowshoes, anything—even though they were not represented in the sample.

Standardization is a long and costly process and must be done several years ahead of the publication of a test. It is usually safe to subtract two to five years from the copyright date to find out when it actually took place. The date is important, because what was considered a representative group then, according to the climate of the times, may not be considered representative today.

For example, the makers of the Stanford-Binet (one of the best of the individually given tests) did not restandardize when they revised the test in 1960 but continued to use what they called "the irreplaceable original standardization sample" of 3,184 white, native-born people collected prior to 1937. To get norms for the new edition of the test, they rescored and reanalyzed the old data gathered over twenty years earlier.

An IQ score is not an absolute measure, like five feet or eighty pounds. Rather, it is your rank in comparison to a certain group of people. The question that the test attempts to answer is not "How smart are you?" but "How well can you compete in this game?" Your opponents are the people in the sample—how do you stack up against them?

Who are these faceless people whose average IQ was arbitrarily pegged at 100? That is obviously the kernel of the matter. If they are truly representative of the whole population, then your score means one thing. If they are not, then your score means something else. And the evidence is irrefutable that they are not representative.

Another misconception is that IQ tests are objective. They are not. They are man-made instruments and inevitably influenced by the judgment of the men who made them.

The usual procedure was for the test maker to pick items, more or less by intuition, and try them out. The criterion was whether they correlated with other estimates of intelligence—that is, would a child who was already considered smart make a high score on this test? If he didn't, those items were discarded and different ones tried.

That other estimate of intelligence was success in school. Because most of the commonly used tests are from twenty to fifty years old (refurbished from time to time), that means success in school *as it used to be*, when schoolwork was booklearning and little else. They are heavily weighted with verbal items and biased in favor of those who have verbal ability.

But schools have changed and are continuing to change more and more all the time. Television, films, and tapes have opened up new avenues of learning. There is no longer the strict reliance on books and printed material that there once was.

The judgment of the test maker is also apparent in his designation of the right answer on multiple-choice items, the sole type of question on most group tests. Suppose a child is faced with this example:

*Aquarium* is to *fish* as *library* is to — — —.
a. bookshelves  b. doors  c. books  d. librarians

It is obvious that *c* is meant to be the correct choice. But looking at it another way, why isn't *d* also a logical answer? Most children, especially in cities, never saw a person they identified as a librarian anywhere but in a library. Therefore, librarians inhabit libraries—fish inhabit aquariums. Besides, fish and librarians are alive—books aren't. But *d* is counted just as wrong as something silly like *a* or *b*.

As is typical of the time when a cult's power is waning, there have recently been a flurry of magazine articles on the IQ. The September, 1971, issue of *The Atlantic* featured a piece by Richard Herrnstein predicting that the ultimate outcome of differences in intelligence (which he claims are largely inherited) will be social stratification and a caste system. But note that throughout he is speaking of intelligence *in terms of scores on present IQ tests.* Translated, what his statement means is that differences in IQ test scores will result in social stratification and a caste system.

Out of the flood of letters *The Atlantic* printed in reply to the Herrnstein article, the one that interested me most was the quiet voice of an insider—a man who for twenty years has worked as a writer of test items. He said, "The question whether race correlates with intelligence really boils down to the issue of how many items can be written which correlate with intelligence but do *not* correlate with race. . . . Unfortunately for black people, most of today's intelligence test items were written long ago." He added that even today he knew of very few blacks employed as test-item writers.

Fifty years ago, when the IQ cult was just beginning to rise, Walter Lippmann, writing in the *New Republic*, November 15, 1922, also referred to an intellectual caste system:

> They claim not only that they are really measuring intelligence, but that intelligence is innate, hereditary, and predetermined. . . . Intelligence testing in the hands of men who hold this dogma could not but lead to an intellectual caste system. . . .

This was part of a heated exchange between Lippman and Professor Lewis Terman, of Stanford University, that exploded into print in the *New Republic*. Lippman wrote a series of six articles described by the editors as "a critical inquiry into the claim, now widely made and accepted, that the psychologists have invented a method of measuring the inborn intelligence of all people." He pointed out that basically the tests were a means of classifying children for the convenience of school administration, and, in the November 15 issue, he said:

> Excellent as this seems, it is of the first importance that school authorities and parents realize exactly what this administrative improvement signifies. For great mischief will follow if there is confusion about the spiritual meaning of this reform. If, for example, the impression takes root that these tests really measure intelligence, that they reveal "scientifically" his predestined ability, then it would be a thousand times better if all the intelligence testers and all their questionnaires were sunk without warning in the Sargasso Sea. One has only to read around in the literature of the subject . . . to see how easily the intelligence test can be turned into an engine of cruelty, how easily in the hands of blundering or prejudiced men it could turn into a method of stamping a permanent sense of inferiority upon the soul of a child. . . .
>
> I do not mean to say that the intelligence test is certain to be abused. I do mean to say it lends itself so easily to abuse that the temptation will be enormous. . . . For the whole drift of the propaganda based on intelligence testing is to treat people with low intelligence quotients as congenitally and hopelessly inferior.

Terman wrote an answering article in the December 27, 1922, issue. As befitted a high priest of the IQ cult, he loftily stated that "The validity of intelligence tests is hardly a question the psychologist would care to debate with Mr. Lippman; nor is there any reason to engage in

so profitless a venture." He didn't deign to rebut Lippmann's points but spent most of the article in ridicule
and satire. Here is a sample:

> [Intelligence testers] have enunciated . . . such
> highly revolutionary and absurd doctrines as the
> following; to wit:
> (1) That the strictly average representative of the
> genus homo is not a particularly intellectual
> animal;
> (2) that some members of the species are much
> stupider than others;
> (3) that school prodigies are usually brighter than
> school laggards;
> (4) that college professors are more intelligent
> than janitors, architects than hod-carriers, railroad
> presidents than switch-tenders; and (most heinous
> of all)
> (5) that the offspring of socially, economically and
> professionally successful parents have better
> mental endowment, on the average, than the
> offspring of said janitors, hod-carriers and switch-
> tenders.

As to the possible abuse of intelligence tests, Terman
said, "Mr. Lippmann does not charge that the tests have
been thus abused, but that they easily could be. Very
true; but they simply aren't. That is one of the
recognized rules of the game."

This head-in-the-sand attitude was answered by a
reader on the correspondence page of the January 17,
1923, issue:

> There is plenty of injustice to be observed by
> anyone who has heard social workers discussing
> their cases. The writer has been in touch with a
> case where a woman's children were taken from

her because she had been tested and found to have "the mind of a thirteen year old child." . . . That there are not other cases, affecting both children and adults, I can neither deny or affirm, but the probability is that there are.

In one of his articles Lippmann had asked how psychologists could say that intelligence was fixed by inheritance when their observations began at four years of age and they had no data on infancy and early childhood. Terman pooh-poohed the idea that an individual's IQ was greatly influenced by what happened to him before the age of four. With heavy-handed sarcasm he said:

> Just to think that we have been allowing all sorts of mysterious, uncontrolled, chance influences to mould children's IQ's this way and that way, right before our eyes. It is high time that we were investigating the IQ effects of different kinds of baby-talk, different versions of Mother Goose, and different makes of pacifiers and safety pins.

In the same vein he went on to suggest that perhaps Mr. Lippmann could get an endowment to set up a "Bureau of Nursery Research for the Enhancement of the IQ." In the light of all the research that has since taken place on exactly this subject, Terman seems to have been pretty far off base in his view of young children. In fact, his habit of referring to a child in terms of his IQ score, as if the child and the score were synonymous, seems to depersonalize children of all ages and lends credence to Lippmann's charge that Terman was insensitive to childhood.

The temper of the times today calls for an overhauling of mental ability tests all up and down the line. The prestigious College Entrance Examination Board is among those advocating innovation. They took a forward step in 1958 when, after nearly sixty years of secrecy, they authorized schools to distribute to students their scores, including those on the Scholastic Aptitude Test (SAT)—supposedly a test of intellectual potential, but like other such tests showing the result of a variety of factors. Each student now gets a booklet of information, with his own scores typed on a gummed label pasted to the front. The booklet explains the scoring system and gives tables showing the performance of various groups—high school seniors in general, high school seniors who entered college, and freshmen at three different types of colleges.

They took a second step in 1967 when they appointed a twenty-one-member commission to make a wholesale evaluation of their testing program. In the current climate of criticism of testing in general, the College Board, like a lightning rod, has drawn a large share of it.

About one-third of the commission members were people who were (or had been) connected with making the tests, another third had been involved with Board activities other than tests, but the rest were outsiders. Included in their number were a member of the editorial board of the New York *Times*, the director of a research laboratory in geophysics, a novelist, and a specialist in computer-assisted instruction. The Board allotted them three years for the project, provided them with a staff and a budget, and left them alone, after promising to publish their report even though it might be critical and an embarrassment.

It turned out to be both. The report (1970), called *Righting the Balance*, pointed out that as things stood, the scales were tipped in the college's favor with the students getting the short end of the deal. The Board is an association of colleges and schools. It serves the interests of, first, the college admissions officer and, second, the high school counselor or principal. The student, essentially a captive and paying customer, is a distant third. His scores are used by others as a factor in making decisions about him—whether he will be admitted to college, whether he will get a scholarship—but the services he receives in return are far smaller.

While the information booklet tells him how his scores compare to those of the students at hypothetical colleges X, Y, and Z, it is of limited help to him in deciding where to apply unless the colleges choose to release information about themselves telling which category their institutions fall in.

Many—but not all—do supply tables in *The College Handbook* listing test scores of the students who applied for admission to recent freshman classes, of students who were accepted, and of students who actually enrolled. In the case of colleges that do not give out such figures, the applicant has to rely for information on a high school counselor with expertise or on the student grapevine, if he is lucky enough to be in contact with either.

To drive home their point, the commission fantasized a situation where the tables were turned and the applicants formed their own association, requiring the colleges to furnish them with information about their institutions using terms and methods that the students stipulated. After all, the student has a right to know what he is letting himself in for when he chooses a certain college. What the commission actually recommended was more reciprocity—a better balance of services among all the parties concerned.

Reinforcing the Board's earlier position that students should see their scores, the commission gave their opinion that "colleges neither need nor should have information about students that is not shared with students for their use." They went even further and suggested that safeguards be set up to protect the student's privacy and that certain parts of the information be released to colleges only if the student gave his permission. This is a far cry from the old days when the colleges got all the information and the student was kept in the dark.

The commission found that what test scores predict is whether a student can make good grades in the standard curriculums as they have usually been taught, by classic methods in traditional subjects, and are no longer suitable for a time when the nature of colleges is rapidly changing.

Today the key word is "diversity." Diversity of students. Diversity of institutions. In 1939 the forty-two colleges that belonged to the Board were Ivy League types, concentrated in the East. Today there are over 850 member colleges scattered all over the country.

Diversity of courses. In addition to the usual subjects, you may now take such things as Buddhism (with a Zen master coming from Japan for a three-day session of contemplation), cinematography, sorcery and witchcraft, the employment of women, African politics (with a six weeks' trip to Africa), Hinduism, introduction to acting, and criminology. According to the *Wall Street Journal*, 200 colleges and universities, including Yale and Princeton, are offering courses in futuristics—the study of the future. For instance, they attempt to answer such questions as "What new kinds of businesses may be needed in the year 2000?" Or they try to predict what marriage will be like fifty years from now by acting out, in simulation games, problems that the twenty-first-century family might face.

To no one's surprise, the commission reported that present tests favor the white middle class. Because the SAT relies heavily on verbal ability, which is tied up with social and ethnic background, they said that if college admissions were based strictly on SAT scores, it would reinforce class and racial biases in American higher education rather than removing them.

They discussed abandoning the SAT (taken annually by more than 1,500,000 students for a fee of $6.50—the major source of the Board's income) but in the end recommended that it be kept if it is considerably modified to be less narrow and rigid. (See Chapter 5 for details of suggested changes.)

The commission operated much like a Senate investigating committee, hearing testimony from many witnesses. In addition to those most directly connected with the college-entrance process—teachers, professors, high school counselors, college admission officers—they included labor union and civil service representatives, an officer of the American Psychological Association, the director of training for the Citizens Crusade Against Poverty, and a well-known critic of the College Board Examinations who has been feuding with them for years on the basis that some of their questions are ambiguous.

After digesting all this testimony, the commission concluded that what was needed was nothing less than a new theory of testing. Research on such a theory has been done in a number of places, but there is as yet no concentrated major effort. Pointing out that the College Board has the resources and the necessary expertise, the commission expressed the hope that it might spearhead a movement to develop tests which measure various learning capacities different from the traditional ones.

A similar call for change has been expressed in other quarters. Lee J. Cronbach, in the preface to the third edition (1970) of his *Essentials of Psychological Testing*, said, "My overall impression of today's practical tests . . . is that they are obsolescent. Tests that saw the light of day before 1949, with new norms and new scoring procedures, are in many areas the best we have today. . . . Is the time not ripe for a wholly fresh effort to construct a new generation of tests?"

Out of the wide variety of approaches tried when testing was young, we have seized on one narrow aspect tied to schools as they were in the past and gone off on a tangent. Today new trends in schooling demand new types of tests. In this book I would like to examine the origins of conventional IQ tests to see how we got in our present position and some of the alternatives offered by new research.

# Chapter 2
## Origins of Intelligence Tests

What is the origin of IQ tests? Where did we get the idea that something as intangible as intelligence can be lassoed, stretched out, and measured numerically?

The first so-called mental tests were given in England almost 100 years ago by Francis Galton, who on his mother's side was a half cousin of Charles Darwin's. They were a by-product of his main interest, the eugenics movement, which he founded.

Galton was the kind of man who is hell-bent on explaining to people how to do things. When he was young he wrote a book explaining how to pitch a tent, how to find water, and other details of camping out. The Crimean War was going on at the time, and Galton offered to give free lectures on the subject to the men at the military training center at Aldershot. The War Office ignored him, but he made a personal application to the Prime Minister, who agreed to his proposal. In spite of the fact that only a few of the trainees showed up for his course, Galton went through with it.

When he was an old man (he lived to be eighty-nine), he wrote a magazine article explaining how to cut a cake according to scientific principles so that it wouldn't get stale. In the fifty or so years in between, he spent much of his energy and time in explaining to people how they should select a husband or wife in order to improve the quality of the human race.

He thought it most unreasonable that horses and dogs are systematically bred to produce a better strain but that humans leave the choice of a mate more or less to chance. His enthusiasm for the cause of eugenics never flagged, although Victorians were no more interested in scientific mating than the Crimean soldiers had been in his course on camping.

If the object is to improve the breed, the first prerequisite is a method of measuring human traits, mental as well as physical, to identify the superior. Galton went to work on the problem and invented a number of tests, together with the apparatus for giving them.

He set up an Anthropometric Laboratory at the South Kensington Museum in London. It was a narrow room with a table full of his paraphernalia on one side so that visitors could file past with the superintendent, taking one test after another. In the six years it was open, 9,337 people were willing to pay threepence each to be measured.

Here are some of the tests he offered:

1. What's the highest of a series of whistles, graduated in pitch, that you can hear? (Galton invented the supersonic whistle.)
2. What's the slightest difference in weight that you can detect among a set of cartridge cases?
3. How far apart must two points touching the skin on the back of your hand be separated in order to be felt as two and not one? (About an inch was considered normal.)
4. What is your reaction time to a. a sound b. a light c. a touch on the skin?

5. How many taps can you make in a half minute?
6. How well can you discriminate among the tints of different colored wools?
7. How much of an angle must there be between two lines so that you see them as two, not one?
8. How many letters can you repeat after one hearing?
9. How good are you at judging with your eye the length of a variable bar?

Notice that instead of testing what we would call sense, Galton tested principally the senses. He was influenced by the belief, current in his day, that because all knowledge comes through the senses, people with the keenest minds would be those with the most acute senses. The importance of his work lies in the fact that he was the first to carry out a large-scale study of individual differences by statistical methods, many of which are still in use.

An American, James McKeen Cattell, was a student of Galton's and for a short time his assistant. When he came back to this country, he brought with him the idea of using tests. At the University of Pennsylvania he made all of his students in experimental psychology take a series of fifty, much like Galton's. He also had a shorter series of ten that he tried on anybody who was willing. When he moved to Columbia University, he took his tests with him. By 1893 he was advocating that tests be given in the schools.

But he soon found out that Galton-type tests did not predict who could, and who could not, successfully do the schoolwork of the period, and they were discarded. Nevertheless, the idea of mental testing, as well as many of the beliefs accompanying it, remained. Like Galton, Cattell thought that intelligence was largely inherited and therefore permanently fixed for life. This philosophy became deeply ingrained in the whole IQ cult and accounted for many of the misuses of intelligence testing.

The IQ tests themselves came not from England but from a grade school on the Rue de la Grange-aux-Belles, a street located in one of the poorer and most populous quarters of Paris. They were the work of French psychologist Alfred Binet and a few collaborators.

Binet was not generally very popular in Paris— he was something of a loner. During his lifetime, his work was not as highly esteemed by most French psychologists as portions of it later came to be in America. Although he was head of the Laboratory of Experimental Psychology at the Sorbonne, he kept the lab open only one afternoon a week and gave no university lectures. He had few students and never went to a scientific congress.

Instead, he spent his time in research— some of it at an institution for mentally retarded children, but mostly in a small lab that he set up at the public school on the Rue de la Grange-aux-Belles. A good description of Binet's lab and the school is given in the article "A Study of the Human Plant" in *The American Review of Reviews*, written in the early 1900's by a Parisian officer of Public Instruction.

The lead photograph, showing some boys being tested, sets the tone of the article— an overriding emphasis on average for age level with everything measured as above or below this average. It is captioned, "These boys are the same age, but of widely different degrees of mentality." Below that, "Three French lads of eleven years of age, whose heads are of unequal volume. Number 1 (at the left) is five years in advance of the normal. No. 2, two years in advance; No. 3, five years behind."

The lab was described as full of apparatus: a series of pieces of wood of varying length, each representing the average height at a certain age; calipers for measuring shoulder width; a steel ellipse that when squeezed in the hand showed the strength of a boy's grip. There was a chart with different sized letters for testing eyesight, like the ones we are used to at the doctor's (except that Binet's had the big letters at the bottom instead of the top), and a net bag of colored wools to see if a child was color blind.

A spirometer (two bottles connected by tubes) measured lung capacity. One of the bottles was filled with water—when a boy took a deep breath and blew through a mouthpiece he forced a certain amount of water into the other bottle, where it was registered in cubic centimeters. The bigger his lung capacity, the more water he could displace by blowing.

When classes in the school were over for the day, some boys came in the lab to be examined. Binet said, "We have sometimes difficulty in keeping them away, so fond are they of being measured and weighed. Yes; we always begin by taking their measurements. The body and the mind are closely united."

While his assistants did the physical measuring, Binet conducted the mental tests. Here are two examples. One was what he called *une expérience d'attention.* Five boys sitting around a table were given a passage from a classical author to read to themselves for ten minutes. Then they wrote as much of it from memory as they could.

"The testing of the memory of each pupil when entering a school is of the greatest importance," Binet said. "What is the good of burdening the memory of a child with twenty lines of verse when he is by nature incapable of ever learning them correctly?"

Another test was of suggestibility. Binet used a piece of paraphernalia made of two cardboard disks—one with a slit through it was superimposed over the other. The bottom disk had lines of various lengths drawn on it and could be revolved in such a way that the lines appeared, one at a time, through the slit in the top disk. For a time the lines got longer and longer, but they finally became invariable. An inattentive child would jump to the conclusion that they always increased, but one who was not so easily taken in would notice the change.

Binet explained his philosophy:

> We have come to see that education is a question of adaptation, and that in order to adapt it to the needs of a child we must make ourselves thoroughly acquainted with his or her mental and physical characteristics. The principle, therefore, that guided me when forming this new laboratory was the knowledge of the average state of development of children of all ages—an entirely new idea in pedagogics.
>
> What my assistants and I set ourselves to find out, in a strictly scientific manner, was the physical and mental value of the average child at various ages. Once having discovered this, we drew up tables of averages. We are able, for instance, to say: "This boy's growth is retarded. Though twelve years of age, he has only the development of a child of nine. He will require special attention and special nourishment. This other scholar, on the contrary, is physically in advance of his age. He is more muscular, taller, and stronger than a boy of ten." A third boy, we note, shows a remarkable mastery over himself, while a fourth is emotional and nervous. One is an observer, calm and calculating; the other imaginative. If the most is to be made out of them in later life, they must be educated differently.

Binet seems to have tried anything and everything that was available for measuring individual differences. The walls of one of his laboratory rooms were covered with framed portraits of children photographed according to the anthropometric system known as bertillonage (after Alphonse Bertillon, the French criminologist of fingerprint fame, who devised it). It was a method of sectional photography in which front and profile views were taken, as well as views of sections of the face that had distinguishing marks and of the convolutions of the ear.

According to the article, once he even called in a Parisian palmist to read the lines in the hands of a hundred boys. Out of all this potpourri, by trial and error he sorted out those methods that served his purpose.

He was commissioned by the Ministry of Public Instruction to devise a test that would separate the true dullards from those who, though failing their schoolwork, had normal ability. Like Cattell in America, he found that Galton's tests were not good predictors of a child's success in school. He abandoned them as too sensory and too simple and struck out in a new direction, experimenting with tests involving judgment, problem-solving, and above all, the ability to understand words and written material.

By 1905 he had assembled a list of tasks—he called them stunts—beginning with those that a young child (or the mentally retarded of any age) could do and ranging upward in difficulty. In his work he had the advantage of comparing normal children at the school where his laboratory was located with mentally retarded children in the hospital at Perray-Vaucluse.

After three years of further experimenting, he was able to group the tasks according to what he thought to be normal age level. In 1908 he and psychiatrist Théophile Simon published their famous test.

Here is a sampling of some of the items in that grandfather of intelligence tests, the Binet-Simon:

## Age Three

1. Point to your nose; your eyes; your mouth.

2. Name the things you see in this picture. (A picture of a man and a boy pulling a cart loaded with furniture.)

### Age Four
1. Are you a boy or a girl?
2. Repeat three digits.

### Age Five
1. Which is heavier? (Two blocks equal in size and appearance, but one weighs three grams, the other twelve grams.)
2. Copy this square.

### Age Six
1. Is this morning or afternoon?
2. What is a fork? a table? a chair? a horse? a mama?

### Age Seven
1. Describe this picture. (Same picture as in age three, but child must describe, not merely name objects.)
2. What's missing in this picture? (Drawing of a woman's face with no mouth.)

### Age Eight
1. What is the difference between wood and glass?
2. Count backward from 20 to 1.

### Age Nine
1. Give me the correct change out of twenty sous. (Play store with real money. Examiner buys something priced at four sous.)
2. Same as Question 2 for age six, but must be defined better than by use—*i.e.*, no credit for "A fork is to eat with."

### Age Ten
1. What's the thing to do if a playmate accidentally hits you?
2. Make a sentence using the words *Paris, fortune, gutter.*

### Age Eleven
1. Where is the nonsense in this sentence, "I have three brothers, Paul, Ernest and myself." (In 1911 revision, Binet moved this to age ten.)
2. Make a sentence out of these words, "A—defends—dog—good—his—bravely—master." (Moved to age twelve in 1911 revision.)

Age Twelve

1. Repeat seven digits.
2. "A person who was walking in the forest at Fontainebleau suddenly stopped, much frightened, and hastened to the nearest police and reported that he had seen hanging from a limb of a tree a — — — ." What was it?

Both of these tasks were apparently too hard and Binet moved them to age fifteen in his 1911 revision and inserted this test on the ability to resist suggestion:

3. Are these two lines equal or unequal in length? (There is a six-page booklet with two horizontal lines on each page. On the first three pages, one line is always longer than the other. On the last three pages, the lines are equal in length. Some children succumb to the suggestion of the first three pages and say that all the pairs are unequal. A child who is not so credulous will notice the change.)

The examiner began with the test corresponding to a child's chronological age or slightly below and progressed upward, ladder fashion, to see how high he could go. His mental age was determined by the highest group of tests he could pass, plus additional credit if he got a scattering of items right in higher tests. (Five additional items equaled one additional year.)

If a nine-year-old could pass the questions on the eleven-year level, it was easy to see that he was above average. But if he could only do the items up through the seven-year-old level, it was also easy to see that he was below. A child was considered mentally retarded if he was more than three years behind.

We eagerly imported the Binet-Simon test and used it in a variety of situations. The notion of mental age—the heart of Binet's scale—was so readily understood by nontechnicians like teachers and doctors that it smoothed the way for acceptance of mental tests. In fact, it was so clear that in at least one case the Binet test was given in open court, with the judge and jury keeping score.

The defendant was a young man who had killed the county jailer in an attempted jailbreak in Rawlins, Wyoming, in April, 1916. But after the murder, he didn't take the keys or make any effort to escape—they found him running around in his cell like an animal.

The defense contended that he had the mind of a child and had been merely the tool of two other prisoners who planned the break and got him to do the dirty work. To prove the point in dramatic fashion, the man's lawyer arranged for a psychologist from Wyoming State University to give him the Binet test in court.

As reported in *The Survey* for January 13, 1917, the psychologist started with the questions for a very young child: "Where's your nose? Point to your eyes," and the like. When he came to "Are you a boy or a girl?" the examiner, in view of the circumstances, changed the wording to "Are you a man or a woman?"

The defendant answered haltingly, "I dunno; I ain't thought much about it." But after the psychologist asked the question again using the standard form, the man said without hesitation, "Boy."

He could repeat only three digits from memory, which on the Binet scale is the digit span of a four-year-old. On all the comprehension questions, the "What's the thing to do if— — —" kind, he invariably said that he would run. Asked what was wrong with the statement "I have three brothers, Paul, Ernest, and myself," he said there was nothing wrong with it.

And so it went throughout the examination. The effect on the jury was powerful—on the first ballot they acquitted him by reason of his mental condition.

To quote *The Nation*, July 9, 1914, "The Binet tests

are all the rage." The prisoners at the Kansas State Penitentiary at Lansing were given the test and 80 percent were pronounced mentally retarded. The same kind of results came from a psychopathic laboratory connected with the Chicago Municipal Court for delinquent youths and for what they delicately called disorderly women.

Reports from other prisons and courts, though somewhat more conservative, also showed a large percent mentally retarded. While Binet expected that his tests would render service in penal cases, in our rush we were using them in a different way from what he intended. His tests were designed as part of a clinical examination. We turned them into a numerical score. He stressed an intensive study of the individual—the relationship between mind and body, the part played by the emotions, a description of the processes used in answering the questions. In all his experiments he put great value on rapport between the examiner and the subject. By merely tabulating answers as right or wrong and overlooking the fact that emotional and other factors connected with prison life could easily cause the low scores, we jumped to a lot of wrong conclusions.

In the schools we coupled Binet's test with the belief of Galton and Cattell that intelligence is fixed and immutable, like blue eyes or big ears. Binet thought differently. In 1909 he wrote that ". . . some recent philosophers appear to have given their moral support to the deplorable verdict that the intelligence of an individual is a fixed quantity. . . . We must protest and act against this brutal pessimism." In short, what happened was that we imported Binet's test but not his philosophy.

There were three translations of the Binet-Simon test well known in this country. The first was by H. H. Goddard, who used it in his work with feebleminded children at the Vineland, New Jersey, Training School.

Goddard, too, was a firm believer in the all-powerful effect of heredity, and his influence gave added support to the creed of a fixed intelligence.

The other two translations were those of Frederick Kuhlmann and Lewis Terman. All three men had graduated from Clark University in Worcester, Massachusetts—at that time a hotbed of psychologists. (Freud made his only trip to the United States at the invitation of the president of Clark and gave five lectures there. Not that intelligence testing and Freudian theories have anything in common, except that both were embraced more enthusiastically here than in any other country in the world. Maybe there's something about Americans that causes us to go overboard.)

Each of the three edited and revised Binet's test to suit his own purpose. Their versions were not identical with each other or with the original. The one made by Terman (1916) had the most impact, and it was Terman whom Walter Lippmann singled out in his *New Republic* series as the leader of the intelligence-testing movement.

After graduating from Clark, Terman, who had tuberculosis, went West on the advice of his physician. In an illuminating sidelight on the medical treatment of the time, Terman said that after his third pulmonary hemorrhage he merely rested for a couple of weeks until his fever subsided and then went back to work. He settled in California, where he joined the faculty of Stanford University. For that reason, his test was called the Stanford-Binet. A revised version is still used today. (See Chapter 3.)

Terman based his test on extensive experiments made by himself and his associates. About 1911 they conducted a preliminary survey of 700 California children, considered their results unsatisfactory, threw them out, and started over. This time they used approximately 1,000 children in California communities of average social status and chosen from schools attended by practically all the children in the district where they were located. He seems to have thought that such a method gave him a representative sampling, although he plainly says that "tests of foreign born children were eliminated in the treatment of results."

Of Terman's 1,000 children, 905 were between five and fourteen years old. The cutoff point was fourteen, because that is the average age of a child in the eighth grade. At that time attendance at high school was far rarer than it is today. So what he had available for his experiments, for the most part, were grade school pupils, and he thanked the many public school teachers and principals who cooperated with him in furnishing the children.

Anybody above the age of fourteen he classified as adult. He had 400 of these—a motley crew made up of 150 hoboes, 30 businessmen, 159 adolescent delinquents, and 50 high school students. Because the teen-agers and the grown men got about the same number of points right on his test, Terman drew the erroneous conclusion that intelligence stopped growing around sixteen. In his 1916 *The Measurement of Intelligence*, he wrote, "Native intelligence, in so far as it can be measured by tests now available, appears to improve but little after the age of fifteen or sixteen years." In the same book, he designated as "average adult" scores falling in the range from fifteen to seventeen years.

Terman was making the same kind of mistake made by some scientists who, observing that middle-aged people walked with their toes turned out and that young people walked with their feet parallel, concluded that the aging process caused them to toe out and that when the young people reached middle age, they, too, would toe out.

But when the group of young people in the experiment grew to middle age, they still walked with their feet parallel. What had happened was that the original middle-aged group grew up at a time when it was thought proper to toe out. In fact, the correct military stance used to be with the feet at a 45-degree angle, as you can see by looking at old photographs of General Pershing and other World War I officers. (Fortunately, podiatrists later found out that this was hard on the arches and it went out of style.) Aging had nothing to do with the way the two groups walked; it was due to a completely different factor.

The only way to tell whether mental powers stop increasing at sixteen is to test *that same group* of people when they are grown. This is what psychologists call a longitudinal study, where the same subjects are retested after the passage of time—in this case, it took a lot of time.

One such longitudinal study was reported in the article "Preschool IQs After Twenty-Five Years" by Katherine Bradway, Clare Thompson, and Richard Cravens in the *Journal of Educational Psychology* (Vol. 49, 1958, pp. 278-81). A group of children between the ages of two and five and a half were given the Stanford-Binet in 1931. They were retested ten years later, when they were between twelve and fifteen and a half, and their average IQ's were approximately the same as before. So far, all was in accordance with Terman. But in 1956, when they were between twenty-seven and thirty and a half years old, a second retest showed that their IQ's had increased an average of 11.3 points. Other longitudinal studies have shown the same thing, but back in the early 1900's Terman's view prevailed.

When he was preparing his test he included for tryout, along with Binet's questions, forty new items originated by himself and others. The first Stanford-Binet, published in 1916, was based almost entirely on the results of his experiments with the 1,000 children and 400 adults in his sample group.

Terman eliminated Binet's question that tested a child's ability to resist suggestion, because it did not correlate with success in schoolwork. Is it possible that it did not correlate because the children who did well in the schools of that day were the suggestible—*i.e.*, docile—ones?

He added a number of his new items, including a vocabulary test on which he set great store. He said, "The vocabulary test has a far higher value than any other single test of the scale," and went on to add that in a large majority of cases the vocabulary test alone would give results within 10 percent of those obtained by using the whole battery.

*The Literary Digest* ran Terman's vocabulary as a sort of do-it-yourself intelligence test in their February 16, 1918, issue, captioned "Of Course You Are a Superior Adult." Terman compiled the list by selecting the last word of every sixth column in a dictionary containing 18,000 words and arranging them roughly in the order of their difficulty. He figured that each word in his list represented 180 words of vocabulary; therefore a person who knew 50 of these would in all probability have a working vocabulary of approximately 9,000 words.

I am sorry that I cannot bring you the list. Houghton Mifflin Company, for test security reasons—*i.e.*, secrecy—refused to grant me permission to reproduce it, saying that they are still using "a great number" of those same words on their current version of the Stanford-Binet. Although I pointed out to them that the list in its entirety was made public in *The Literary Digest*, that virtually every library in the United States contains bound volumes of the old issues of that magazine, and that many have Xerox machines handy where, for a dime, anybody who wants to can run off a copy, they remained adamant.

If you want to try a comparable vocabulary test, I

suggest you use a dictionary and pick out 100 words the same way Terman did. Here are the scoring standards as given in the magazine article:

| Words Correct | Mental Age |
|---|---|
| 20 | Eight years |
| 30 | Ten years |
| 40 | Twelve years |
| 50 | Fourteen years |
| 65 | Average adult |
| 75 | Superior adult |

It was Terman who coined the phrase "intelligence quotient" and made the two juxtaposed letters *IQ* as much a part of the language as *OK*. The German psychologist William Stern had already suggested that instead of subtracting a child's chronological age from his mental age, as Binet had done, it would be better to divide them, giving the ratio of the two. Ratios are very revealing. For instance, suppose you grow a half inch overnight—probably few people would notice it. But if your nose grew a half inch overnight, everybody would notice it. It's a half inch in both cases, but its relationship to your height is very different from its relationship to the length of your nose.

The same principle is involved in Terman's ratio IQ's. Suppose a ten-year-old child is two years ahead—that is, his mental age is twelve. The answer (or quotient) when 12 is divided by 10 is 1.2. Multiply by 100 to get rid of the decimal, and the child's IQ is 120.

But suppose it is a five-year-old who is two years ahead, with a mental age of seven. Using the same method of figuring, his IQ is 140. Each child is two years ahead of normal, but the relationship of that two years to the older child's age is quite different from its relationship to the younger one's age.

These ratio IQ's obtained by dividing the chronological age into the mental age were used for a number of years, then replaced by a different method of computation (explained in Chapter 3). So ingrained was the 'IQ concept by that time, however, that the old name stuck, although, strictly speaking, the score was no longer a quotient. The Stanford-Binet test was among the last to abandon Terman's method, but even they switched in their 1960 revision.

Terman laid great emphasis on the numerical score. He believed that the IQ stayed fairly constant throughout life and therefore adult intelligence could be predicted in early childhood.

Not only did he have great confidence in the ability of his test to ascertain the IQ, but he and a Stanford associate, Catherine Cox, purported to find the IQ's of a group of 300 people who never took a test and furthermore had long been dead. Napoleon, they said, had an IQ of 145. Lincoln's was 150. Goethe scored 210.

They didn't merely say that these people must have had high IQ's, a reasonable statement, but assigned each a fairly exact number: Da Vinci, 180; Galileo, 185. How anybody could swallow as scientific fact something that was obviously speculation is amazing. But such was the awe in which the IQ was held, the aura surrounding the whole process, that their study was solemnly received.

The Binet tests were given in Berlin, Brussels, Breslau, Rome, Petrograd, and Moscow, as well as in England and America. By 1920 there were at least twenty-four revisions of the original Binet-Simon scale. Among other things, the author of each revision decided at what age level each task belonged, judging from experiments with his own selected group of children.

Did they all find the same things "normal" for the same age? Positively not. Terman shifted twenty-five of Binet's items to a younger age, one of them by as much as six years younger. He moved four items to an older age group, leaving only nineteen where Binet had placed them.

From Cyril Burt's book *Mental and Scholastic Tests*, we can trace the peregrinations of a specific item. For example, the examiner asks, "What is this color?" as he touches in turn four pieces of paper—one each of red, blue, green, and yellow. Originally used for eight-year-olds, Binet himself changed this to age seven in his 1911 revision of his scale. In the three American versions, Goddard left it at seven, Kuhlmann moved it to six, and Terman said a normal five-year-old could do it. Elsewhere, it was variously placed at ages four, five, six, and eight.

The only items that all experimenters agreed on were in the test for three-year-olds. All the others fluctuated by anywhere from one to nine years. The difference, of course, stemmed from the makeup of the group of children that each man chose and on which he based his verdict of what was "normal."

Here is plain evidence of the importance of the standardization group. It is quite possible that if a child's answers were judged by the performance of one reviser's group he would be called mentally retarded, but those same answers weighed against another reviser's group would be classified as normal. Contrary to popular belief, there was no universal scale. Nor is there any universal scale now, although for the past fifty years we have tended to act as if there were.

# Chapter 3
## Individually Administered Tests

Before World War I, IQ tests were always given to one person at a time. Group tests didn't come until later. An individual test, administered in a face-to-face session by a trained examiner, has always been considered more accurate and reliable, but it can be expensive. School psychologists do not charge for testing the small percentage of children referred to them for special study, but if you go to a private psychologist, the cost may run to $100 or more.

Many parents do take their children for private testing—in fact, in some circles it's a sort of status symbol. But the bulk of its use outside schools is in clinics, both the tax-supported and the privately endowed variety, where the tests are employed for adults as well as children. If the clinical psychologist thinks that the trouble is educational or neurological, he will probably want an individual IQ test.

There are two individually administered tests that are far more widely used than any others—the Stanford-Binet and the Wechsler Intelligence Scales. Which one is largely a matter of the examiner's personal preference. A typical choice would be the Stanford-Binet for little children up to seven or seven and a half, the Wechsler after that. What are these tests like?

The present Stanford-Binet is a direct descendant of the one described in the preceding chapter. In 1937 Terman and Maud Merrill, also of Stanford, revised it to conform with the results of ten years of research. The most obvious change was that everything was bigger—more tests, more items per test, more people in the standardization sample.

One of their aims was to make two complete and comparable forms of the examination, so that a child could be retested after a short interval without repeating the same questions. They collected literally thousands of potential new items that looked as if they might test whatever it is that IQ tests test and tried them out on subjects in the vicinity of Stanford whose IQ's were already on record. Out of this preliminary sifting, they chose enough new questions that, combined with the old ones, gave them two forms each with approximately 200 items (later whittled to 129). Every person in the standardization sample took both these forms, administered not less than a day or more than a week apart.

The standardization sample itself was made up of 3,184 people—over twice as many as Terman had used twenty years earlier. They were chosen from all over the United States and an effort was made to get a representative selection according to fathers' occupations, urban or rural residence, etc. But again, as in Terman's first group, all were white and all were native born. In fact, in half the cases both parents were also native born—the children were second-generation American.

Because the testing was done in the Depression years of the thirties, it was easy to get school pupils up to the age of eighteen. Since there were few jobs available, more adolescents stayed in school through high school, instead of leaving to go to work at the end of the eighth grade as had been the common practice when Terman took his first sample.

This time the difficulty was at the other end of the scale—getting enough preschool-age children to test. (Their sample ran from age two through age eighteen.) In one community, they asked parent-teacher associations and ladies aid societies to supply the children, but they turned out to be so untypical (average IQ 112) that the whole group had to be eliminated.

A better method was to use the younger brothers and sisters of school pupils already in the sample. In cities there were also children available at day nurseries, well-baby clinics of the city health centers, and the like. But in small towns where no such resources existed, the most productive technique was to write a letter to the mother explaining the purpose of the study and asking her cooperation, then follow this up by a telephone call or personal visit. Most mothers agreed, although about 3 percent refused to allow their children to be tested because they "didn't believe in it," "were not interested," "were too busy," "it was inconvenient," and so on.

By trial and error, Terman, Merrill, and their Stanford associates hammered out their two complete tests— Form L and Form M. In 1960 it was further refined by taking the most discriminatory items from both of the 1937 forms and combining them into a single scale. This revision is the one currently in use.

It is an omnibus of twenty tests, covering every age level from two years to adults. They are spaced at six-month intervals for the younger children (up to five) and at yearly intervals thereafter. With a few exceptions, each test is made up of six tasks and one alternate in case something goes wrong.

The paraphernalia for giving the test fills a briefcase. It includes dolls, beads, blocks, household items in miniature, scissors, toy locomotives, an American flag, a tiny shoe, and pictures, as well as printed material for older children and adults.

To give you the flavor of the tests, here are some of the tasks for two-year-olds:

1. An infant version of the old shell game. There are three small empty boxes and a little toy cat. While the child watches, the examiner hides the cat in one of the boxes. Then he puts a screen in front of the boxes and keeps it there for ten seconds. He removes the screen and tells the child to find the kitty. (The first box the child picks up is the one that counts.)

2. Identifying parts of the body on a large paper doll—a cherubic, Kewpie-looking little white boy.

3. A picture vocabulary of eighteen common objects. The examiner points to each in turn, saying, "What do you call this?" Two-year-olds are expected to get three right.

The material is lavish. An identical cat is used in a task for four-year-olds, but there are two cats in the set, just alike except for the color of their collars. There are also three toy dogs, each for a separate test, and three toy automobiles. (True, one is glued to a card with some more objects, but the other two could be interchangeable.)

At the opposite end of the scale, to gain a rating of superior adult, you must be able to do things like this:

1. Give the meaning of certain proverbs. (One out of two is passing.)

2. Solve three arithmetic problems of the kind that are usually called thought problems or word problems. They must be done mentally within a timed interval of three minutes per problem.

3. Repeat the thought of a short paragraph that is read to you.

In between these two extremes, here are a few items selected at random. Three-year-olds get a picture memory test. First the examiner shows a card with a single picture on it. "What's this?" The child says that it's a cow ("moo-cow" is acceptable). Then the examiner takes the card away and shows a second card with the same cow surrounded by pictures of a lot of other things. From remembering the first card, the child has to pick out the cow—the examiner is careful not to say what they are looking for.

Four-and-a-half's get something much like the *Sesame Street* song that says: "One of these things is not like the others. One of these things doesn't belong." It's called pictorial similarities and differences. For instance, a card has three squares and a circle on it. Which one doesn't belong with the others? There are five cards altogether—passing is three cards right.

The Stanford-Binet is heavily loaded with items where a knowledge of words is essential. Five-year-olds have to define three common words. Seven-year-olds are asked how pairs of common objects are alike. Thirteen-year-olds rearrange a string of scrambled words to make a sentence. A full-scale vocabulary test appears at many levels, from six years up.

There are 117 different tasks all together. Some of them are used more than once, at different ages. For instance, a comprehension test asks what the child should do in six common situations. An average seven-year-old is expected to get three right, an eight-year-old to get four.

Nobody takes all 117 items. The Stanford-Binet is a ladder-type scale, each rung corresponding to a mental age. The examiner ordinarily starts a little below the child's chronological age and works up, rung by rung, to find the highest test on which he gets all the answers right. From this base they proceed upward, until they reach the child's ceiling—a test where he fails all the tasks.

Mental age is computed by starting with the base age and adding a certain number of months for each higher task that is passed. For example:

| Test | Items Correct | Credit |
|------|------|------|
| Five Years (Base age) | All | 5 years |
| Six Years | 3 | 6 months |
| Seven Years | 1 | 2 months |
| Eight Years | 1 | 2 months |
| Nine Years (Ceiling age) | 0 | |
| Total | | 5 years 10 months |

Usually a young child can be tested in thirty to forty minutes, an older one may require an hour and a half because his successes and failures normally scatter over a wider range of age levels. It may take seven or eight complete year levels before finding his ceiling, and each level has six separate items. Once a child starts on a rung of the ladder, he must try all the tasks, even when it is obvious that he doesn't understand. (The essence of a standardized test is that it must always be administered in the same way, otherwise the score is not comparable to the norm.)

This means that in the latter part of the examination he is being asked quite a lot of things that he cannot do. Although the examiner usually tries to reassure him by saying, "I didn't expect you to get them all," or words to that effect, most children know when they're getting them wrong and find the experience frustrating.

It is especially true of a child who shows a self-depreciating attitude, like the seven-year-old who early in the test said, "I can't draw very well." Unlike some children who immediately take all the materials in their own hands before starting, she waited passively to be handed each piece. Although nobody had asked her to read anything, she volunteered, "I can't read very well."

Attempting encouragement, the examiner said after a success, "My, do you do this well at school?" After a string of failures, "I know this is going to make your mother happy when I tell her how hard you worked." Notice that these statements imply approval without saying whether the answers are right or wrong, which would be against the rules.

When the child obviously became more and more discouraged, the examiner tried to end the session on a happy note by ad-libbing a question that everybody can get. "If you had three magic wishes, what would they be?" Since this came after the test was officially over (although the child didn't know it was), it did not un-standardize the procedure.

The content of the test is beginning to show its age. All the items in the present version are taken from the two forms of the 1937 test; no new material was added. Only the pictures of an airplane, a ship, and a telephone were redrawn in an effort at updating. They still show, as something familiar to all children, a picture of a work-man wearing bib overalls and using a handsaw.

In one of the tasks for four-and-a-half-year-olds, called aesthetic comparison, the child is given a card with pictures of two girls on it and asked to say which one is prettier. There are three of these cards— two with pairs of girls, one with a pair of boys. In each case, one of the pair has classic features, including a straight nose. The child gets a plus if he picks these as prettier. Of the "uglier" member of each pair, two have very broad, flat noses, the third has a high-bridged, hooked nose.

There are certainly ethnic objections to an illustration of this kind. If it were offered in a textbook today, it would be called bigotry. It also seems to be rather naïve to assume that it is a mark of intelligence to consider certain ethnic features pretty and others ugly.

A few of the questions appear to center on deportment rather than mentality—for instance, one that asks for reasons why children should not be too noisy in school. The manual, which gives carefully worked out lists of acceptable and unacceptable answers, includes "They'll have to sit in the dunce chair" as acceptable. (How long has it been since schools had dunce chairs?)

The whole idea of mental age, so useful when intelligence testing was new, is becoming outmoded. For one thing, it tends to give the impression that two children with the same mental age have the same kind of mind. This is not true. If a seven-year-old and a twelve-year-old each have a mental age of ten, they both got the same number of items right but probably not the same items. They arrived at their scores by different paths. In all likelihood, the bright younger child earned his credits on tasks requiring analysis and judgment, the dull older child on tasks based on factual information that comes from schooling or experience.

At the adult level the concept of mental age is meaningless and is just a computational device leading to an IQ score. The Stanford-Binet starts all adults off with fourteen years' credit and adds months according to the following scale:

Average Adult Test—2 months for each correct item
Superior Adult Test I—4 months for each correct item
Superior Adult Test II—5 months for each correct item
Superior Adult Test III—6 months for each correct item

Since no one over eighteen was included in the 1937 standardization sample, their adult norms are merely projections and hence rather shaky. This test has also been criticized because the adult ceiling is not high enough for the exceptionally talented to show their ability. Binet's test was designed principally for children, and that is where it is strongest. At the adult level, most psychologists prefer the Wechsler, which was developed first for adults and then extended downward—the reverse of the Binet.

The Wechsler tests were published by the Psychological Corporation, an organization sometimes called the Tiffany of mental testing. When it was started, it was probably the only American business firm that required all its stockholders to have doctorate degrees. The company enjoys a reputation for frankness of reporting, even to the extent of listing in the manual instances where a test had failed to do what it was supposed to do.

The Wechsler Intelligence Scales were originally developed by David Wechsler out of his experience as a clinical psychologist at Bellevue Psychiatric Hospital in New York City. His tests differ from the Stanford-Binet in two major ways. First, instead of being constructed by age levels, all subjects take the ten subtests. Second, half of these subtests are verbal and half are performance; therefore it is not so heavily weighted with verbal items as the Stanford-Binet. There is a separate IQ score for each of these two categories, as well as a combined IQ for the test as a whole.

The same characteristics run through all three of the Wechsler scales—the adult test, the one for children five through fifteen, and the one for preschoolers. The middle one, the Wechsler Intelligence Scale for Children (WISC), published in 1949, is the one most used in schools. A look at some of its details will give you an idea of what all the Wechsler tests are like. Here are the ten subtests:

| Verbal | Performance |
|--------|-------------|
| 1. General Information | 1. Picture Completion |
| 2. General Comprehension | 2. Picture Arrangement |
| 3. Arithmetic | 3. Block Design |
| 4. Similarities | 4. Object Assembly |
| 5. Vocabulary | 5. Coding |

Alternates

| | |
|--|--|
| 6. Digit Span | 6. Mazes |

The content of the verbal half of the test is similar to the Stanford-Binet but in general is more compact. For instance, questions on similarities—*i.e.*, "How are an orange and an apple alike?"—are all concentrated in one subtest. The Stanford-Binet has at least four scattered subtests involving similarities, ranging in age level from seven years to superior adult.

It is interesting to compare the two vocabulary tests. The WISC has 40 words; the Stanford-Binet, 45. No word appears on both lists. Judging from the scoring tables given in the two manuals, children at each age level know more of the WISC words than they do of the Stanford-Binet's. For example, an average eight-year-old knows 8 words on the Stanford-Binet scale, but he knows the equivalent of 11 to 12 words on the WISC. A fourteen-year-old knows 17 words on Stanford-Binet, 22 to 23 on the WISC.

Does this mean that the WISC vocabulary is easier? Possibly. A more likely explanation is that it is because of the WISC method of scoring by points, which allows a child to get partial credit if he shows even a vague knowledge of a word's meaning. Two words half right would be the equivalent of one word exactly right. On the Stanford-Binet there is no partial credit. All answers are scored either plus or minus, with nothing in between. (Binet himself suggested giving one-half or even one-fourth credit to children's answers on many parts of his tests, but this practice was abandoned in the American translations.)

In the WISC performance section, the picture completion test is a series of twenty cards, each with a picture of an object—a comb, a cow, a rooster, and so on—with some part missing. For instance, the comb is minus one tooth. The child gets fifteen seconds to look at each card and detect the missing part.

The picture arrangement test is like a cartoon strip with the order of the panels shuffled. The child has to rearrange them so they tell a story. (*Sesame Street* often has games like this. Children must be getting smarter. When Wechsler was adapting his scale for preschoolers, he had to omit this kind of test because the task couldn't be explained adequately to young children.)

Perhaps the most noteworthy of the performance tests is the block design, a measure of analytic ability unencumbered with words. It uses a set of nine identical blocks, each with one side painted red, one white, one blue, one yellow. The other two sides are divided diagonally into a pair of triangles—a red and white pair and a blue and yellow pair.

The examiner shows the child a card with a colored design on it—for instance, a chevron—and asks him to duplicate it with his blocks. They start with easy patterns using only four blocks and progress to harder ones calling for all nine blocks. The test is scored for correctness and speed, but it also gives information about the child's natural style of problem-solving. Since all the designs are red and white, does he begin by turning these faces up on all the blocks and then assembling them? Or does he start at one corner and build up the pattern a block at a time? These are matters of personality rather than intellect but are important in understanding how each child learns.

The object assembly test consists of four jigsaw puzzles made of camel-colored board—a manikin, a

horse, a face, and an automobile. The child is to put each
of these together within a specified time. The horse, for
example, must be done within 180 seconds. He gets
bonus points for speed and also partial credit for getting
even two of the pieces of any puzzle together correctly.

Object assembly is the only part of the WISC where
the child has to try all the test, no matter what. On all
the others, provision is made for discontinuing a subtest
after a certain number of consecutive misses. Also,
normal children eight years old or more can skip the first
few questions in most of the subtests and automatically
receive credit for them. These two devices cut down the
total time required, so that the WISC can usually be
given in about an hour.

Wechsler abandoned the mental age as a basic
measure of intelligence. He used a different technique of
computation that showed only how a child compared to
others of the same age. Ten-year-olds were rated in
relation to other ten-year-olds— nothing was said about
what an eleven-year-old could do.

Because this method is now standard on most intelligence tests, here is a good place to explain it. And it
needs to be explained. All most laymen know is that the
child is closeted with the psychologist, who comes out
with a number score— the IQ.

Where does he get this number? To be honest, what he
does is to count up the points the child got right on the
test, giving what is called a raw score, and then he looks
up this raw score on a conversion table in the manual to
get the IQ. But where did the numbers on the conversion
tables come from, since there is no mental age to divide
by the chronological age, as in the old IQ method?

The statisticians who made the tables did two things.
First, they found the average raw score of all the
children of a given age— say ten years old— in the
sample. (Wechsler had 200 ten-year-olds in his sample.)
Whatever this average was, they arbitrarily converted it

to 100. Second, they looked to see if the raw scores of the 200 children in the sample clustered close to the average or if they differed by sizable amounts. Using a statistical computation that I won't go into, they arrived at a sort of standard amount by which all the ten-year-olds' raw scores deviated from the average. This standard deviation, whatever it was, they arbitrarily converted to 15. They did the same two things for each age level.

Their arbitrary numbers—100 for the average and 15 as the standard deviation—were purposely chosen to result in IQ's similar to those figured by the old method, so that the body of lore built up over the years wouldn't be disturbed. People by that time were so accustomed to receiving reports in terms of an IQ of 95 or of 125 that it was like pulling eyeteeth to get them to change over to other numbers. In fact, some test makers tried changing and soon found out that to appease their clients they had to provide a measure that resulted in numbers in the familiar range. That is the reason for the arbitrary choice.

This method assures that approximately two-thirds of all IQ scores in the sample will fall within one standard deviation of 100—that is, between 85 IQ and 115 IQ. This is the middle group. About 95 percent of all scores will fall within two standard deviations of 100, in the range from 70 to 130 IQ. Three standard deviations in each direction from 100 will take in practically everybody in the sample. The scores are not evenly spaced but cluster together in the middle and thin out toward both ends in the normal distribution curve used in much statistical work.

(To clear up any possible later misunderstanding, let me say here that the Stanford-Binet, when they finally switched to this method, used 16 as their standard deviation.)

Some of the content of the WISC is open to criticism. Theoretically, an aptitude test is based on experiences that all children have. But are these? The test on general information certainly discriminates against children from culturally disadvantaged environments. How likely is a child from an impoverished background and poor schools to pick up information about Genghis Khan or Romeo and Juliet in his day-to-day living, no matter how intelligent he is?

As far as that goes, how much experience have urban and suburban children had with cows? Enough to know that their hoofs are cleft? What used to be a common experience for a large segment of the population no longer is. After all, not many zoos have cows in them.

The WISC, as well as the Stanford-Binet, does seem to be still rather cow-oriented. The WISC used the 1940 U.S. Census as a basis for selecting the children in their standardization sample. That census showed 42.1 percent rural. Shifting population patterns in this country have caused the rural percentage to steadily decrease ever since. In 1950 it was 36; in 1960, 30.1; in 1970 it had dropped to 26.5 percent.

The Wechsler tests are designed in such a way that it is possible to compare not only a person's verbal IQ with his performance IQ but also his subtest scores with each other. Wechsler believed that the pattern formed by the highs and lows of the different subtests could be used in diagnosing certain psychiatric cases. He even worked out a formula for identifying schizophrenics, but it did not stand up under study and is no longer used.

However, this separation of scores on different subtests has encouraged the setting up of clinical hypotheses about psychopathic character disorders—for instance, that a conspicuously high score on picture arrangement indicates a shrewd schemer, or that if a picture completion score is well above the other parts of the test it shows overalertness and watchfulness. These inferences are not substantiated by research, and psychological theory has made many advances since

Wechsler designed his tasks. Such a use of the Wechsler Intelligence Scales is not valid.

Roughly speaking, validity means "Does the test do what it is intended to do?" A test may be valid for one purpose but not for another. Both the Stanford-Binet and the WISC were valid predictors of success in schoolwork *as the schools were when these tests were made.* Whether they are for the schools of today is another question.

They are not valid for a number of other uses to which they have been put, especially as a measure of native intelligence in the ongoing argument about heredity vs. environment. Binet explicitly stated that what he was measuring was a complex of several factors, including the amount of opportunity that the child has had, both in school and out, of learning some of the things called for in the tests. He pointed out that this depends partly on the curriculum of the child's school, and he laid special emphasis on the opportunity relative to language and vocabulary.

Besides validity, the other trait invoked in judging a test is reliability. Both the Stanford-Binet and the WISC rate high, but when statisticians in the field of psychometry use the word "reliable" it has a special meaning, different from its everyday use. In psychometrics, "reliability" means "repeatability." An elastic ruler is not reliable because you could measure the same line with it several times and get a different answer every time. A more stable ruler has greater reliability—that is, you get approximately the same answer every time you measure that line.

The reliability of tests is checked by either of two methods. One, used by Stanford-Binet, is to test the same children on two different forms. They gave Form L and Form M of their 1937 test to the same group less than a week apart and compared the results. The other is the split halves method, used if no alternate form is available. The makers of the WISC figured the children's scores on all the even-numbered questions and on all the odd-numbered questions separately and compared the two.

But suppose the stable ruler has a built-in bias. It has repeatability, all right—every time you measure you come out with that same bias. There is evidence that, like the Stanford-Binet, this is the case with the WISC. They used a standardization sample of 2,200 children carefully apportioned by sex and age—100 boys and 100 girls for each year, five through fifteen—chosen from eighty-five communities in eleven states. They were correctly distributed according to father's occupation and rural-urban residence to match the percentages of the 1940 U.S. Census, except for 2.5 percent of the sample who were known to be feebleminded and were in institutions. But all 2,200 children were white.

It is futile to use scores from either the Stanford-Binet or the WISC to compare IQ's of different races, because only one race was represented in their standardization samples. Furthermore, the validity of many group tests was established by correlating their scores with those on one or the other of these two outstanding individual tests, passing the same bias along to them.

If a child takes a Stanford-Binet today and the WISC tomorrow, will he come out with the same IQ on both? Probably not. Aside from small differences due to the vagaries of scoring, luck, how he feels on the day of the test, and the like (each has a standard error of 5 IQ points, meaning that an IQ score of, say, 104 really represents a band running from 99 to 109), they do not measure exactly the same abilities. The verbal section of the WISC is rather closely related to the Stanford-Binet. According to studies made in the 1960's, the correlation is .80 (perfect correlation is 1.00). But the WISC performance section correlates with the Stanford-Binet to a lesser degree—.65.

These same studies also showed that on the average normal and superior children tended to score higher on the Stanford-Binet than on the WISC, but in the case of the dull the reverse was true. This fact led Cronbach, in *Essentials of Psychological Testing* (1970), to conclude that "Evidently one test or the other was standardized on an unrepresentative sample, but we have little basis for judging which is at fault."

Each contains tests of a type not included on the other, but for the considerable area where they overlap, here are some details of the way each handles them:

| STANFORD-BINET | WISC |
|---|---|

### Vocabulary

| | |
|---|---|
| 45 words. Answers scored only as plus or minus. No partial credit. Child is shown card with words printed on it. Stop after six consecutive misses. (This is only test where child may stop without trying all of it.) | 40 words. Answers scored 2, 1, or 0, allowing for partial credit. Child is not shown card and gets no credit if he defines homonym. Stop after five consecutive misses. |

### Similarities

| | |
|---|---|
| Includes some differences along with similarities— that is, how are two things alike and how are they different? Scored as passing of failing according to criterion for age level. Passing may be two items out of four, three out of five, three out of three, etc. | Analogies and similarities combined into one test of sixteen statements. Stop after three consecutive misses. |

### Comprehension

| | |
|---|---|
| Child presented verbally with various situations and asked what he would do. Also questions on why so-and-so. Scored passing or failing according to criterion for age level. | Same type of questions as Stanford-Binet, but scored 2, 1, or 0, allowing for partial credit. Stop after three consecutive failures. |

## Arithmetic

Problems on reasoning and ingenuity must be done without pencil or paper.

Time limit varies from 1 to 3 minutes per problem.

Scored passing or failing according to criterion for age level.

16 problems, some read to child, some on cards for him to read.

Each problem has time limit varying from 45 seconds to 120 seconds.

Stop after three consecutive failures.

## Digit Span

Scattered among tests for various age levels. Sometimes digits must be repeated forward, sometimes backward.

Youngest children get three trials—1 trial right is passing.

Used as alternate test only.

Test in two parts—digits forward and digits backward.

Two trials for each question.

Score is highest number of digits right.

## Picture Completion

Includes mutilated pictures and picture absurdities—that is, picture complete, but with something wrong with it.

Scored passing or failing according to age criterion.

20 cards, arranged in order of difficulty. Each shows an object with something missing. Child can look at each picture for 15 seconds.

Scored 1 point for each correct response.

Stop after four consecutive failures.

## Mazes

Only given at one age level. Child tries 3 mazes.

2 right is passing.

May be used instead of coding test, at examiner's discretion.

Several practice mazes provided, then five different mazes on test proper.

Time limit on each, ranging from 30 seconds to 120 seconds.

Stop after two consecutive failures.

# Chapter 4
## Invention of Group Testing

The Russell Sage Foundation published a survey, *Experiences and Attitudes of American Adults Concerning Standardized Intelligence Tests* (1965), that turned up some interesting statistics. Men take more IQ tests than women do. A larger proportion of political Independents reported taking tests, and taking more of them, than either Democrats or Republicans. Seventy-nine percent of people sixty-one or older never took an intelligence test. Going down the line, age bracket by age bracket, the percentage of adults who have taken IQ tests climbs steadily. The rise is smooth, except for a big increase when we come to those now in their fifties.

What happened around fifty years ago that caused this sudden jump in test taking? It was the invention and subsequent popularization of the group IQ test. That's the kind that touches most of us—in school, in applying for a job, in the military, or maybe all three.

World War I spawned the group IQ examination. The Army wanted a quick way of identifying, at one end of the scale, about 5 percent of the recruits to put into officer training and, at the other end, of eliminating the feebleminded from the ranks. They carried out the testing in characteristic military fashion.

Between 100 and 200 men were ordered to report at a time. After a five-minute literacy test, those who couldn't read or write English were withdrawn and the rest were supplied with pencils and printed forms of the Army Group Examination Alpha.

A senior officer stood at the front of the room and read the general directions through—once only. After a few preliminaries outlining the purpose of the tests, the *Examiners' Guide* instructed him to say, "When I call 'Attention!' stop instantly whatever you are doing and hold your pencil up, with your elbow on the table. Don't put your pencil down to the paper until I say 'Go.' Listen carefully to what I say. Do just what you are told to do. Ask no questions. As soon as you are through, pencils up. . . . Don't turn any page forward or backward unless you are told to."

What were the tests like? During the war they were a military secret—revealing the contents was punishable by a $10,000 fine, a two-year prison term, or both. However, the March, 1919, issue of *The American Magazine* carried what they called a specimen set, saying that it paralleled the actual tests very closely. Here are three of their samples, published under the heading "Try These Tests on Yourself and Others":

1. With your pencil make a dot over any one of these letters F G H I J, and a comma after the longest of these three words: boy mother girl. Then, if Christmas comes in March, make a cross right here. . . . but if not, pass along to the next question, and tell where the sun rises. *East* If you believe that Edison discovered America, cross out what you just wrote, but if it was some one else, put in a number to complete this sentence: "A horse has . . . feet." Write yes, no matter whether China is in Africa or not. *Yes* ; and then give a wrong answer to this question: "How many days

are there in the week?". 5... Write any letter
except g just after this comma, √ and then write no
if 2 times 5 are 10. Ν.Q Now, if Tuesday comes after
Monday, make two crosses here. XX ; but if not,
make a circle here. ... or else a square here. ...
Be sure to make three crosses between these two
names of boys: George XXX. Henry. Notice these
two numbers: 3, 5. If iron is heavier than water,
write the larger number here. ..., but if iron is
lighter write the smaller number here. ... Show
by a cross when the nights are longer; in summer? ... in winter? X. Give the correct answer to
this question: "Does water run uphill?" ... and
repeat your answer here. ... Do nothing here
(5+7=..12. ), unless you skipped the preceding
question; but write the first letter of your first
name and the last letter of your last name at the
end of this line: Ν Ζ

The test above takes the average adult 125
seconds. Fifty percent of average educated adults
come somewhere between 100 seconds and 150
seconds. To take less than 100 seconds is to be in
the superior 25 percent. To take more than 150
seconds is to be in the poorest 25 percent. If people
are divided into Excellent, Good, Fair and Poor,
Excellent will be anything less than 100 seconds;
100 to 125 will be Good; 125 to 150 will be Fair,
while over 150 will be Poor.

2. north      sick       tall
   sour       slow       open
   out        large      summer
   weak       rich       new
   good       dark       come
   after      front      male
   above      love

Look at each word in the test, see what it means, and call out the word that means just the *Opposite* to each word. The score is the time in seconds, with no errors. The average adult record is 25 seconds. Below 21 seconds is Excellent, 21 to 25 seconds is Good, 25 to 29 seconds is Fair, over 29 seconds is Poor.

3.

8 - 3
6 - 4 - 1
2 - 8 - 5 - 4
3 - 1 - 7 - 5 - 9
5 - 2 - 1 - 7 - 4 - 6
2- 1 - 8 - 3 - 4 - 3 - 9
7 - 2 - 5 - 3 - 4 - 8 - 9 - 6
9 - 5 - 4 - 2 - 3 - 7 - 1 - 8 - 6

Have someone read the numbers to you, at the rate of one digit a second. (In the Army, the officer giving the test read one row of figures aloud to the group, paused for ten to fifteen seconds while the men wrote down as much as they could remember, then read the next row, paused, and so on.) When they have finished a line repeat the numbers in the same order as read. This is a test of immediate memory. The average adult can remember 7 numbers. More than 8 is Excellent, 7 to 8 is Good, 6 to 7 is Fair, below 6 is Poor.

The Army examinations were prepared by a seven-man committee headed by Robert Yerkes, who was made a major in the newly established Division of Psychology in the Surgeon General's office. Yerkes' reputation was chiefly in the field of animal psychology— he said himself that he was made chairman of the committee only because he happened to be president of the American Psychological Association that year (1917).

Two translators of Binet's test, Terman and Goddard, were on the committee. Furthermore, Terman's pupil at Stanford, Arthur Otis, had been working on the construction of a test that could be given to groups instead of individually. Otis turned his material over to the committee, and with some alterations and additions, it was adopted.

Six weeks after the committee first met, their test sheets and report blanks were ready for the printer. They made a trial run under working conditions, using 4,000 men already in the armed services and comparing their scores with the officers' ratings of the men. A few more revisions, and group intelligence testing of recruits got underway at four national Army cantonments: Camp Devens (Massachusetts), Camp Dix (New Jersey), Camp Lee (Virginia), and Camp Taylor (Kentucky).

Next, the War Department extended intelligence testing to the entire Army, excepting only field and general officers. By January, 1919, a total of 1,726,966 men had taken the tests at thirty-five Army training camps.

Jelled into final form, the Army Group Examination Alpha had eight parts as follows:

Test 1— Comprehending and Carrying Out Directions
Test 2— Arithmetic Problems
Test 3— Practical Judgment (Common Sense)
Test 4— Synonym-Antonym (Same and Opposite)
Test 5— Disarranged Sentences
Test 6— Number Series
Test 7— Analogies (Word Relations)
Test 8— General Information

Scores were not expressed as IQ's, which at that time were figured by dividing chronological age into mental age— a method that makes no sense for adults. While we all agree that a four-year-old is usually more advanced in every way than a three-year-old, it doesn't follow that a man who is twenty-four is necessarily more advanced than one who is twenty-three. (In fact, the results of the Army's test showed no correlation between a soldier's score and his age.) Instead, they were given in points scored out of a possible 212 for getting every answer right. (Nobody did.) The highest was reputed to be a 207 made by an officer who was a Yale professor in civilian life. Anything approaching 200 was rare. Here is the Army's rating scale:

| Points Right | Ranking | |
|---|---|---|
| 135-212 | A | Very Superior |
| 105-134 | B | Superior |
| 75-104 | C+ | High Average |
| 45- 74 | C | Average |
| 25- 44 | C− | Low Average |
| 15- 24 | D | Inferior |
| 0- 14 | D− | Very Inferior |

An *E* rating was reserved for those considered unfit for duty because of mental inferiority and discharged (about one-half of one percent).

The seven-man committee who constructed the Army tests thought at the time that they were measuring inborn intelligence. W. V. Bingham, the secretary, in a 1917 press release explaining the program, said, "The aims of the entire psychological examination are to measure native intelligence and ability, not schooling; to disclose what a man can do with his head and hands, not what he has learned from books. . . ."

Hindsight suggests otherwise. Whatever they were measuring, it seems to have been closely bound up with the amount of schooling a man had had. A graph of data from Yerkes' *Psychological Examining in the United*

*States Army* (1921) giving the distribution of Alpha scores according to previous education shows a predominance of college men at the upper end of the scale, with the bulk of those who had not advanced beyond grade school concentrated in the middle and lower end. But we believe what we want to believe, and in the 1920's the leaders of the IQ cult were in the driver's seat. A vital part of their mystique was that their intelligence tests could ferret out native ability— something very deep, lasting, and quite different from a school examination.

Because the Alpha required the ability to read questions on a printed sheet, illiterates and non-English-speaking recruits took a different test, the Army Beta, that was constructed in such a way that the directions could be given mostly in pantomime. There was a blackboard at the front of the room, with the same figures painted on it that were on the test blanks. The officer in charge tapped the blackboard, pointed to the question sheets, picked one up and held it next to the black-board—in general, trying to convey the idea that what his assistant did on the blackboard the men were to do on their papers.

Test 1 was a maze. The assistant demonstrated by tracing through the sample maze on the blackboard with a piece of chalk. When he purposely went into a blind alley and crossed over a line, the officer shook his head vigorously, said, "No, no," and took the demon-strator's hand back to the place where he could get on the right track again.

He held up a test blank, traced an imaginary line with his finger through each maze on the sheet, and (according to the *Examiners' Guide*) said, "All right. Go ahead. Do it. Hurry up." There was a great deal of emphasis on speed. Orderlies walked around the room, motioring to men who were not working and telling them to "Do it. Do it. Hurry up, quick."

The other parts of the Beta examination were:

Test 2—Cube Analysis (Pictures of cubes stacked
up so some at the bottom or rear of the pile were
hidden from view by those in front. How many
cubes in each pile?)
Test 3—Analyzing Patterns of O's and X's
Test 4—Coding
Test 5—Matching Two Columns of Digits
Test 6—Incomplete Pictures
Test 7—Geometrical Figures

Scores were expressed as points out of a maximum of
118. Here are the Army's letter ratings for the Beta:

| Points Right | Ranking |
|:---:|:---:|
| 100-118 | A |
| 90- 99 | B |
| 80- 89 | C+ |
| 65- 79 | C |
| 45- 64 | C— |
| 20- 44 | D |
| 0- 19 | D— |

The Beta was a forerunner of the nonlanguage, so-
called culture-fair tests used today. Theoretically, it did
not require the subject to understand English, but a look
at the way the directions were given suggests why it
was not as successful as the Alpha.

The Army used test scores in several ways. The
commanding officers in certain corps issued orders that
candidates for officers' training school must have an A,
B, or, in some cases, C rating. This policy was later
changed and the obligatory feature removed, making
intelligence scores only one of the chief factors to be
taken into consideration.

In some camps the recruits were divided into four groups according to their test results. One major who had done this went out on the drill field a week later to see if he could tell which platoons were made up of men with an A intelligence rating, which with a C, and so on. He said that he had no difficulty in picking out the best (A and B), the medium (C), and the lowest (D) platoons but couldn't see any difference between the A's and the B's.

Very low scores were commonly made the basis for assigning men to labor battalions. Beginning in May, 1918, they were also the basis for putting men in special development battalions for intensive training to see if ways could be found for using them in the Army.

All went well until, after the war, the Army's point scores were translated into mental age levels and the results made public. According to the scales and the method of calculation then in use, it turned out that the average Army draftee had a mental age of approximately fourteen years.

There was much screaming and hand-wringing over the low quality of American brainpower. The furor spread from coast to coast and even washed over into England, where the *Lancet*, after interviewing Cyril Burt, psychologist to the London County Council, concluded that the British didn't have anything to be smug about, if the same scales were applied there.

What the figure actually showed was the danger of applying to 2,000,000 men a theory that was in the experimental stage, with the bugs still in it. The next rung after the test for fourteen-year-olds on the Stanford-Binet ladder is the one for adults. Therefore, there was really only one year's difference between the mental age of fourteen and the beginning of the average adult level at fifteen. We have already seen that many of the tasks in the Binet test were relocated at other age levels in the various revisions of the test around the world. After the

Army results were made public, some psychologists
proposed that Terman's "fourteen-year" test be renamed
"average adult" test, but he did not take kindly to the
suggestion.

Under attack, Terman said that the translation of the
Army scores into mental ages did not rest on the
standards embodied in his Stanford-Binet scale at all. He
pointed out that mental age standards for the Army
were established by giving both the Alpha and the Beta
to groups of schoolchildren and setting up parallels
between their scores and those of the draftees.

Here is a classic case of the tail wagging the dog.
Compared to the size of the Army, the number of
children tested was very small. The figures could just as
easily have been interpreted to mean that as far as Army
test scores went, average fourteen-year-old students in
school did as well as or a little better than the average
soldier. (It is not surprising that they should, since the
tests reflected the subject's past educational op-
portunities. The average fourteen-year-old student is in
the eighth grade. A very large number of World War I
draftees had less schooling.)

Put that way, there would have been no uproar. It was
the phrase "mental age," plus claims that the psychologists had invented a scientific way to measure the
hereditary intelligence of all people, that caused the
trouble.

The awe and unquestioning faith that the intelligence
testing process inspired shows in this excerpt from *The
American Magazine* (March, 1919). The article "How
High Do You Stand on the Rating Scale?" refers to a
fictitious lieutenant, Ralph Jones (the italics are mine):

. . . There is no divergence of opinion concerning
Ralph among the army officials in Washington.
They do not guess about him; they do not classify
him with any such vague terms as "good" or

"mediocre" or "poor." They know precisely where he stands in relation to every other officer of similar rank in the army. *By scientific tests they have measured his mind and rated his abilities. . . .*

How has the army in so short a time arrived at so precise an estimate of Lieutenant Jones' capacities? How is it possible for his military employers to agree so exactly concerning him, when his employers in civil life were so far apart? The answers to those questions are very important to any man who expects either to be an applicant for a position or to pass upon the application of other men in the next few years. They constitute one of the big contributions which are to be made to the future of business by the world war.

It was enough to scare the daylights out of anybody applying for a job. The idea took hold that, by some mysterious method, a printed test could probe the dimensions of a man's mind and come up with a precise measure of its capacity in the same way that the capacity of a two-gallon jug could be measured. Furthermore, like the jug, his mental capacity was determined at the time he was made and was unalterably fixed for life. The test pasted the label on him for all his prospective employers to see.

Business firms that employed many people did adopt intelligence testing. The invention of the group test took the IQ out of the lab and the clinic and put it in the personnel office.

It also put it in the classroom on a large scale. The War Department released the Alpha for civilian use in 1919, and a number of colleges tried it on their entering freshmen— Oberlin, University of Illinois, University of Iowa, Dickinson College, Brown University, Purdue, and Southern Methodist University at Dallas, to name a few. By 1920, some high schools were using it.

Whenever it was given to mixed groups, males out-scored females on the average, by about ten points. Of course, the Army Alpha was constructed as a man's test, by and for men. (Might not our present situation, where blacks take tests made by white psychologists for a predominantly white population, have a parallel here?)

The men picked up most of their advantage on Test 8 (General Information), which was based on masculine experience. Sample question: Where is the Packard Automobile Company's plant located? They also con-sistently beat the women on Test 2 (Arithmetic), although by a much smaller margin. Scores by sex on the other tests were close together, with women making their best showing on Test 3 (Common Sense), Test 5 (Mixed Sentences) and Test 7 (Word Relations).

New group tests were soon forthcoming. The extent to which the IQ test was sweeping the education world can be gauged by this excerpt from a speech made at the Chicago 1920 convention of the American Association for the Advancement of Science:

Custom dictates that this address shall concern itself with some recent and important application of scientific methods to educational problems. . . . There can be little doubt that the outstanding feature of the past year or two has been the interest in intelligence tests and their uses. . . .

That intelligence tests have "arrived," so far as the school is concerned, I had proof positive several weeks ago when representatives of two prominent book companies came to my office, not, as I ex-pected, to recommend their latest text-books, but to extol the merits of the latest intelligence tests. What better evidence is needed that tests are here as a force to be reckoned with than that book companies are rivalling in their production? Of the making of many intelligence tests there is no end.

There certainly wasn't—and for a boom market. Just think of the sales potential for inexpensive, convenient tests that could be administered to large groups of people by examiners who needed no special qualifications. Most group tests are sufficiently self-explanatory so that the examiner simply passes out the forms and directs the subjects when to start and stop.

Both Terman and Otis became editors for the World Book Company (whose president was a Stanford alumnus) and held their positions for many years. Testing had already turned into big business, spurred by the advertising that the Army examinations gave it. In the field of education alone, according to the speaker quoted above, by 1920 there were nineteen different group tests available and 700,000 children had taken one or the other of them.

# Chapter 5
## Use of Group Tests in School and Industry

In the light of Arthur Otis' major contribution to the Army Alpha, it is not surprising that he was the first to come out with an IQ test developed for the burgeoning market in the schools. The *Otis Group Intelligence Scale* was published in 1918 by the World Book Company (later Harcourt, Brace & World, now Harcourt Brace Jovanovich). Riding on the tremendous flood of publicity from the Army's testing program, it went through three printings between March and September, totaling 500,000 copies. By December, a fourth large printing was necessary to supply schools that wanted to test pupils at midyear.

Terman nudged any reluctant educators onto the bandwagon with this statement in the 1921 manual:

Thanks to the use of such tests in the United States Army, their experimental period is a thing of the past. It would be surprising to find teachers and school principals lacking in that open mindedness toward psychological methods which was so conspicuously present in army officers.

A succession of tests followed—the Otis General

Intelligence Examination: Designed Especially for Business Institutions, the Otis Self-Administering Tests of Mental Ability, the Otis Quick-Scoring Mental Ability Tests. They were all very popular.

The most recent revision is the Otis-Lennon Mental Ability Test (1967). Since the Otis tests are among the best known and most widely used in the group field, a look at this one will give you an idea of today's typical school intelligence test.

It is available on six levels, from kindergarten all the way up through high school. Let's take a middle one, the Elementary II, Form J, designed for the fourth, fifth, and sixth grades, as an example. It's given to a whole class at once, in the classroom by the teacher— no special qualifications are needed to administer the tests, the publishers say. Working time is forty minutes, not counting the time for distributing materials, filling in the name of student, date of birth, etc. If the test is going to be scored by machine (as in all likelihood it will be), these preliminaries are no easy task.

Say you are a fifth-grader handed a test blank. On the front there is a row of 16 boxes to print your name in— last name first, first name last, with an empty box between. Englebert Wilkershire becomes "Wilkershire Engl." But a machine can't read printing, so you also have to blacken in the correct oval out of a vertical column of 27 ovals (one for each letter of the alphabet and one for blanks) over each box.

The procedure is similar for your birth date. "Record the last two digits of the year of your birth in the boxes on the left edge of the grid, the third digit in the first box and the last digit in the second box." Be sure to get the year and month right, or your report will come back with the wrong IQ, because it's based on how you stand compared to others your age. And be neat, because the electronic eye can't tell an accidental smudge mark from a mark you really mean. The same goes for the test questions—make your answer marks heavy and dark and fill the space completely. If you change your mind, erase every bit of the first mark. One boy said, "Filling out the front is the hardest part of the test."

### Practice Examples

Sample **X**

**Eye** is to **see** as **ear** is to –
**a** head    **b** hear    **c** talk    **d** nose    **e** cheek
The right answer is choice **b** "hear" so a mark has been made in the answer space under **b** in answer row **X** of the Sample Answer Spaces.

Sample **Y**

A boy bought 3 pencils at 5¢ each. How much did the 3 pencils cost?
**f** 5¢    **g** 10¢    **h** 20¢    **j** 25¢    **k** none of these
The right answer, of course, is 15¢. Since this answer is not given, choice **k** "none of these" is correct. See how the answer space under **k** in row **Y** has been marked.

Sample **Z**

◯ is to ◯    as    ☐ is to –

**a** ☐    **b** ☐    **c** ◯    **d** ◯    **e** ▭

The right answer is choice **a** so the answer space under **a** in row **Z** has been marked.

Reproduced from Otis-Lennon Mental Ability Test, copyright © 1967 by Harcourt Brace Jovanovich, Inc. Reproduced by special permission of the publisher.

There are 80 questions, arranged roughly in order of increasing difficulty. Analysis shows that 37 of them are purely and solely about words, 28 are on numbers or geometric figures, and 15 are miscellaneous forms of reasoning, 9 of which are imbedded in sentences. So are 5 of the number problems (see Sample Y). That leaves 29 that might be called nonverbal, but even for these you have to be able to read the directions in order to answer them.

The largest single category is the ubiquitous verbal analogy, like Sample X. This is the most universal of all items on group IQ tests. If there is one ability you are lost without, it's the ability to do analogies. One test-weary boy said, "I'm so tired of questions like 'Hand is to glove as foot is to— — —' " and he was only in the eighth grade at the time. If it's not done with words, it's done with shapes, like Sample Z.

Since they are all multiple-choice questions, the perennial question is If you don't know the right answer, should you guess? In general, and within limits, yes, although the odds vary from one test maker to another. The *Otis-Lennon Manual* very helpfully tells you, "Do not guess blindly, but you may mark an answer even when you are not perfectly sure that it is right. Your score will be the number of questions correctly answered." In other words, there is no penalty for guessing wrong. A mistake is no worse than a blank.

Some tests are scored in such a way that you are penalized for wrong answers, but even so, an educated guess (not the eenie, meenie, minie, moe kind) is usually to your advantage. The only drawback is that you may waste time in guessing and never get to questions near the end of the test, some of which you may know.

Incidentally, if neither the test booklet nor the manual says anything about guessing, it is against the rules of a standardized test for the examiner to give any supplementary advice. "Standardized" means that the test is meant to be given under uniform conditions, with exactly the same directions read in all schools. Otherwise, the scores cannot be compared to the norms. Of course, everybody knows that complete uniformity is impossible to achieve and that many teachers don't go by the rules. I'm just telling you what the theory is.

If the tests aren't sent away to be graded by machine, they can be hand graded. The teacher merely lays a stencil, furnished by the publishers, over the child's paper and counts the number of answers that show through the correct holes. This raw score tells you nothing until it is converted into a standard IQ by the method described in Chapter 3 for the Wechsler individual tests.

In addition to an IQ, the Otis-Lennon, like most other group tests, also reports the score in percentile form—a way of showing where the child ranked in comparison to other children. For example, if he is in the sixty-second percentile, it means that he either beat or tied 62 percent of the children his own age in the standardization sample.

Accustomed as we are to thinking in terms of number grades, 62 sounds low. If he made that on a spelling test we would be upset. But in percentiles the meaning is entirely different—the sixty-second percentile is actually above average and quite creditable. Those who rank exactly in the middle of the group are in the fiftieth percentile.

Percentiles have the advantage of being easy to understand, once you get used to them. And it's important to know when a score is being reported in percentiles and when it isn't. I know people who have come away from a conference with their child's counselor quite depressed because he made an 85. They thought his *IQ* was 85. A *percentile* score of 85 is very good and something to be proud of.

A mother whose fifth-grader was in the ninety-second percentile was dismayed. "That's the same score as last year. He hasn't improved any."

Of course he had improved. Last year he was higher than 92 percent of the fourth-graders. If he had stood still, he would be in a much lower percentile—maybe the forty-second—when compared to fifth-graders.

Any form of ranking is like a horse race: It only has significance when we know something about the competition. A horse that comes in tenth in the Kentucky Derby is superior to one that comes in first in a field of platers. For percentiles to have meaning, you have to know something about the test maker's standardization sample to which all scores are compared.

According to the *Otis-Lennon Manual,* their basic sampling unit was the school system, chosen according to size, type, social and economic background, and geographic region to correspond as nearly as possible to the United States school population in 1965. The kit of materials sent to the 117 participating schools asked teachers to administer the tests exactly as specified in the directions, so that the results could be used in establishing national norms.

The Primary Level tests for kindergarten and first grade are highly verbal, even though they require no reading. They are made up entirely of pictures and geometric designs. But roughly half of each test calls for the children to follow specific directions read by the teacher at fifteen-second intervals for each problem. For example, she says to mark the picture that shows two boys running, or to mark the circle with the biggest star in it. The manual warns against explaining the meaning of any word, because this is partly a test of vocabulary.

There are many difficulties in trying to give group tests to five- and six-year-old children. They are easily distracted and have very short attention spans. Often they are not motivated to do well on tests. Since they can't read, even page numbers have to be replaced with pictorial symbols. The teacher says, "Find the page with the little horse at the top," instead of "Turn to page three."

No matter how much she says about not helping each

other on the test, and no matter how far apart she seats
the children, there's always one who gets up, runs over
to another child, and says, "That's not right. Scribble
that out. Mark the biggest star."

Teacher, "Shhhhhhhhhh."

Child, "But Mrs. Woods, that's what you said."

The other part of the test consists of rows of four
objects each—three of them alike in some way, the other
one different. For example, there may be three dogs and
a box. The teacher says, "Look at the row of pictures
next to the little bird. Find the picture that is different
from the others and circle it." Fifteen-second pause,
then, "Look at the row of pictures next to the kitten.
Find the picture that is different from the others and
circle it." So on, twenty-three times. After about the fifth
one, some children begin to zip on through, circling
answers without waiting for directions.

Teacher, "Stay with me. You'll do a better job if you
stay with me."

Child, "But, Mrs. Woods, you keep saying the same
thing over and over."

Or they stop and fold their arms. Teacher, "No, no,
we're not finished. There are a few more to do."

Child, "I don't want to do this anymore. I'm tired of
this."

One kindergartener said, "I hate this. If I'd known you
were going to do this I'd never have come. I'd have gone
straight to first grade." (Little did he know that the same
thing was waiting for him there.)

Groups have to be small—a dozen or so—to get any
kind of results, and even then they are undependable.
Some schools don't give intelligence tests at all until the
third grade. The *Otis-Lennon Manual* advises that on the
Primary Level tests the score for any pupil who doesn't
get over 15 questions right, out of a possible 55, should
not be recorded and the child should be given an individually administered mental ability test.

The Advanced Level, for high school, is very similar to the Elementary II but harder. This level has also been used in industry. Like other general ability tests, it is under fire because of the 1970 Supreme Court decision in the Duke Power Company case. The court's ruling made it plain that it was up to the employer to show that the tests they gave job applicants were directly relevant to the jobs they were applying for. The NAACP and representatives of other minority groups charge that such tests when used for hiring and promotion discriminate against minorities and tend to keep them frozen on the lowest rung of the employment ladder.

The employer with the largest number of employees is government at all levels—local, state, and federal. They, too, are affected by the Supreme Court decision. To take a concrete example, Tulsa gives the Advanced Level of the Otis-Lennon to the applicants for its Police Department. Jim Hardy, an industrial and governmental test writer in charge of testing for the Personnel Department of the City of Tulsa, said, "The Supreme Court is going to hit the Otis-Lennon hard in employment situations unless there is good reason for using it. Employers have got to be able to prove that their tests correlate with the skills needed for the job, or they are in trouble."

Hardy validated its use for the Police Department by comparing candidates' scores on the Otis-Lennon with their final grades earned at the end of their training course at the Tulsa Police Academy—A, B, C, or D. He divided the men into two groups, those whose Otis-Lennon raw score was above 55 (out of a possible 80) and those who were below 55. Eight times in a row, for eight successive graduating classes, he found that the average Police Academy grade for those in the upper group was significantly higher than the average made by those in the lower group.

In validating a test for a specific use, Hardy pointed

out that it is important that the data be for the group that is naturally involved in taking the test—for instance, that they are all applying for clerical jobs. He said, "In establishing norms, you hear all the time that a sample of one thousand cases is better than a sample of one hundred cases, but this is not necessarily true. If there are scores there that don't belong—say, twenty out of the thousand are applying for jobs as sanitation workers—it will affect the results."

Hardy said, "The great enigma in personnel testing is why minority groups do less well. The difference is not racial, it's cultural. If you grow up in a family where learning is not very important, there is a natural cultural barrier—it doesn't make any difference what color you are. Suppose a man has a good record on the job, then at thirty-two he faces a test for promotion. He doesn't want to take it—thinks the test is unfair. And it may be, or it may not. But when you can develop the feeling that a test is something that must be prepared for, with everybody studying the same things using the same guidelines under free competition, then it is possible to lower the cultural barriers."

He thinks the solution lies in having not a test but a testing program that includes counseling. For example, thirty days in advance of the police corporal promotional examination he puts out a sheet outlining the material that will be covered and giving concrete study suggestions. For example, on Nature and Use of Evidence they are, "Know the rules of evidence and the proper procedure for evidence preservation, testifying in court and the use of original notes." For Municipal Police Administration, "All questions will be taken from Chapters 6, 7, 8, 9 of the 1969 edition of *The Municipal Police Administration Book* published by the International City Managers' Association." Under Patrol Methods and Techniques, "Read Chapter 5 on Police

Patrol Administration. Review first-aid procedures." For the last four years, blacks' average scores on this examination have been almost identical with the whites' average.

As an example of what can be done about the problem of minority groups and IQ tests in general, Hardy took on privately, after working hours, the case of a young Mississippi black who had applied for a job for which such a test was a prerequisite. His score was so low as to be practically nonexistent. "All that indicated was that he didn't know how to handle the test," Hardy said.

The man could read all right—that wasn't the trouble. Working with him for an hour or so a day, three to five times a week, Hardy used the key-word concept. For instance, in the question What is the color of grass? the key words are "color" and "grass." Over and over Hardy had him read questions. "Al, what are the key words?"

Then they looked at the possible answers: 1. Yellow 2. Green 3. Blue-green 4. Red. Hardy said, "Most grass is green. Some, like Kentucky bluegrass, is blue-green. In the fall, sometimes grass is yellow. But it is never red, so we can eliminate red." Al understood.

"I want you to look for the answer that tells how it is most of the time. When we think of grass, most of the time we think of green grass. So the answer is green. That's the way I want you to think."

He deliberately chose examples that included things that were sometimes possible, but he stressed that the right choice was the answer that was *most* acceptable *most* of the time. After six weeks of this, Al took the test again and made an IQ score in the 95-105 range.

The culture factor in IQ testing in the schools has been much discussed and there have been many attempts to devise a test that would circumvent it. These so-called culture-fair or culture-free tests usually call for the recognition of relationships among figures and designs.

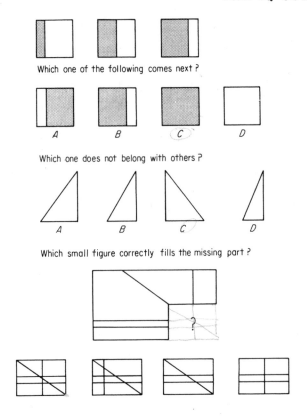

Which one of the following comes next ?

Which one does not belong with others ?

Which small figure correctly fills the missing part ?

The heavily verbal slant of conventional tests is eliminated, which is an advantage, but it is impossible to do away with other, more subtle cultural differences. There is the difference in motivation—for the disadvantaged child, the test is often something unpleasant, to be gotten through with as quickly as possible. He checks answers at random—anything just to get through with the chore.

An extreme effort to avoid cultural bias is a mechanical contrivance invented by John Ertl, director of the Center of Cybernetic Studies at the University of Ottawa. Utilizing a computer and a football helmet with two electrodes inside that rest on the subject's head, it measures the speed with which his brain waves respond to a flashing light. Ertl calls it a neural-efficiency analyzer and makes no claim that it measures intrinsic intelligence but, he says, neither do traditional IQ tests. (Is this maybe a space-age version of Galton's tests, especially the one on reaction time to a light, mentioned in Chapter 2?)

In addition to the *Otis-Lennon* another well-known test that had its roots in the boom period after World War I is the College Entrance Examination Board's Scholastic Aptitude Test. Today the SAT is given all over the world. You can take it in San Francisco or in Keflavik, Iceland; in Chicago or Addis Ababa; Paris, Texas, or Paris, France—it's all the same to the College Board. If there is no test center within seventy-five miles of you, they even offer to set up one if possible.

The SAT was first given in 1926. Like the other tests of that period, it came out of the experience of psychologists who had participated in developing the Army Alpha. Previous College Board tests had been examinations in specific subjects—English, chemistry, etc. The SAT was an attempt to measure a student's power to learn, rather than his knowledge of a certain field. Because then, as now, aptitude for academic work was often mistaken for general intelligence, the Board issued a warning along with the test: "Any claims that aptitude tests now in use really measure general intelligence or general mental ability may or may not be substantiated." It appears that the warning was largely ignored.

Unlike the usual IQ test, the questions on the SAT are continually changing. Each edition has its own life cycle, with new ones being produced and old ones retired at the rate of about four a year. The Educational Testing

Service—one of the largest test publishers and a non-profit organization—constructs the exams. Their staff is always at work devising new items, and it also has been their custom to buy questions from a pool of writers—former employees, professors, and the like—who make up test items in their spare time.

They need so many because the SAT is given five times a year, a different edition each time. Security measures to prevent any advance knowledge of a test's contents from leaking out are stiff and account for a large part of the cost of the SAT. Prospective employees of the Educational Testing Service are screened. Contracts with outside printing companies have security clauses. Every copy is counted when it comes from the printer and counted again at each testing center. If copies disappear, that's the end of that edition's usefulness.

The SAT usually beings at 8:30 on a Saturday morning on the same date all over the world. The only exception is for students whose religion prohibits their taking the test on a Saturday, in which case they may arrange to take it on the following Sunday. To enter the testing center, everybody must show an admission ticket and some other identification—driver's license, Social Security card, or the like.

The SAT takes three hours of working time and is in two parts, verbal and mathematical. Here are three examples of questions from the verbal section:

## Analogies*

CISTERN: WATER: (A) shower: cloud (B) Official: power (C) science: matter (D) museum: antiques (E) vault: valuables

*All examples are from *A Description of the College Board Scholastic Aptitude Test, 1971-1972,* published by the College Entrance Examination Board, New York. Reprinted by permission of Educational Testing Service, the copyright owner of the sample questions.

Sentence Completions

As warfare has come to engross an increasing proportion of the belligerent populations, so military— — —has grown far beyond the problems of varying terrain.
(A) custom (B) life (C) history (D) strength (E) geography

Antonyms (Opposites)

COMPOSURE: (A) analysis (B) alertness (C) contrast (D) agitation (E) destruction

There are also items on reading comprehension, where several passages taken from a variety of fields are given, followed by questions on each. In the College Board's opinion, the ability to read with insight and understanding is so important that half the testing time for the verbal section is devoted to this part of the exam.

Here are three examples from the mathematical section:

Standard Multiple Choice Questions

The town of Mason is located on Eagle Lake. The town of Canton is west of Mason. Sinclair is east of Canton, but west of Mason. Dexter is east of Richmond, but west of Sinclair and Canton. Assuming they are all in the United States, which town is farthest west?
(A) Mason (B) Dexter (C) Canton (D) Sinclair (E) Richmond

The houses on the east side of the street are numbered with the consecutive even integers from 256 to 834 inclusive. How many houses are there on the east side of the street?
(A) 287 (B) 288 (C) 289 (D) 290 (E) 291

## Data Sufficiency Questions

*Directions:* Each of the data sufficiency problems below consists of a question and two statements, labeled (1) and (2), in which certain data are given. You have to decide whether the data given in your statements are *sufficient* for answering the question. Using the data given in the statements *plus* your knowledge of mathematics and everyday facts (such as the number of days in July or the meaning of *counterclockwise*), you are to black space

A   if statement (1) ALONE is sufficient, but statement (2) alone is not sufficient to answer the question asked;

B   if statement (2) ALONE is sufficient, but statement (1) alone is not sufficient to answer the question asked;

C   if BOTH statements (1) and (2) TOGETHER are sufficient to answer the question asked, but NEITHER statement ALONE is sufficient;

D   if EACH statement ALONE is sufficient to answer the question asked;

E   if statements (1) and (2) TOGETHER are NOT sufficient to answer the question asked, and additional data specific to the problem are needed.

In a four-volume work, what is the weight of the third volume?
(1) The four-volume work weighs 8 pounds.
(2) The first three volumes together weigh 6 pounds.

Many of the mathematical questions may be done by a long, a medium, or a short way. For instance, in the second example above, you could simply count the houses up—certainly a time-consuming method. A quicker way would be to figure that there are fifty even-numbered houses in each complete block—in this case blocks 300 through 700—making 250, then count only the two partial blocks and add the whole thing up. The quickest way is to subtract 256 from 834, divide by two, and add one.

All these methods give the answer 290, which is correct. But someone who consistently chooses a long or medium way will, quite obviously, not get as many problems done in the alloted time limit and therefore will end with a lower score.

After the examination is over, a lot of people are perturbed to find that one section of questions is not the same on everybody's test. (It is especially unsettling if a student who is strong verbally has drawn an extra math section, and vice versa.) But they don't need to worry. The variable section is experimental and doesn't count on their scores. That's how new items are tried out for future tests. The Educational Testing Service takes a randomly selected sample of papers and compares a student's performance on the regular test with his performance on the experimental section. If a trial item is answered correctly by most high-scoring students but missed by most low-scoring students, then it appears to be a good item because it differentiates. An item that almost everybody gets right is not, because it doesn't.

The SAT is penalty-graded—that is, something is subtracted from your score to counteract the answers you may have gotten right by guessing. For questions like the examples above with five choices the correction formula is the number of rights minus one-fourth of the wrongs. Suppose, out of 55 questions, you get 35 right, 12 wrong, and leave 8 blank. Three points (one-fourth of 12) are subtracted from your right answers—your final raw score is 32. On the other hand, if you leave a question blank, nothing is subtracted. This is meant to discourage wild guessing, but it doesn't pay to be too cautious. If you can narrow the possible answers down by eliminating one or two that you know are wrong, then the odds swing in your favor and you will benefit from judicious guessing—provided, of course, that you don't waste too much time over it.

Results are reported separately for the verbal and math parts on a scale unlike that of any other test. Scores run from 200 to 800, with 500 being the middle of the standardization sample, which was made up of college applicants in 1941. Because the questions are continually changing, they use a test-equating method to peg 500 on any particular test at the raw score that would have been earned by the average 1941 applicant had he taken this test.

Therefore, 500 is not the average of all people who take the SAT today. In fact, the average score on the verbal section made by high school seniors (many of whom don't go to college) is about 375. Five hundred *is* the average of those who go on to graduate from college with a baccalaureate degree—a rather select group. Incidentally, girls and boys have roughly the same average scores on the SAT, unlike the Army Alpha.

The purpose of the SAT, purely and simply, is to help admissions officers predict how applicants will do in college. Used in combination with high school grades, it has in the past usually predicted about two-thirds of their freshman grade averages within half a letter. But that was when it was used principally by the Ivy League and their imitators. The 900 colleges that now require it are far more diverse, and many Ivy League colleges are leaders in the curriculum reformation now being thrashed out.

The SAT is considered to be very narrow. It measures chiefly verbal and mathematical abilities, with predominant emphasis on the verbal. These are abilities that a candidate has *developed*—slowly and over a long period of time. They are to a large extent dependent on long-term education and therefore have been denied to certain disadvantaged groups.

The College Board's Commission on Tests felt that ways to identify other abilities are needed. For example, in many departments the formerly ubiquitous term paper has given way to the project, with the results turned in on film or tape. Talk to a man who has taken drugs with aborigines, go out and sample the air or water for pollution, ride around on a raft in Georgia photographing what you see. None of these things is dependent on the reading and writing skill that was formerly the underpinning of success in college.

Here are some of their concrete proposals aimed at breaking out of the present rigid mold and making the SAT more flexible:

1. Have a whole battery of tests of a number of abilities that are needed in different forms of education. Colleges could then choose the tests that suit their own purpose. The goal would be to reveal the educational potential of students who have not had the advantage of a good education in conventional terms.

2. Attempt to break the stranglehold that verbal ability has on the present SAT by having one test showing how well a student can comprehend language and a separate test showing how well he can reason with material already understood. It would be more predictive for those without educational advantages.

3. Administer some parts of the SAT as listening comprehension tests, to give a fair chance to students with reading difficulties. (Books and printed material are no longer the only source of knowledge. Many college courses use tapes, television, films, etc.)

4. Reduce the speed element by using fewer items per test.

5. Do away with multiple-choice questions altogether and substitute free response by using computers, like the computer-assisted instruction programs now in effect in some places. The student could enter his response quickly and the computer would tabulate it.

This last proposal was made by David Tiedeman of Harvard, the chairman of the commission. While it boggles the mind to picture 500,000 students at a computer network, all inputting their answers to SAT questions (what would they do in, say Bangkok?), it shows the lengths to which some people are willing to go to get away from the stereotyped examination. As Tiedeman said, you can't expect different types of answers if the types of questions remain the same.

# Part II
# An Alternate Path

# Chapter 6
## Alfred Binet and Jean Piaget

Let's go back to the work of Alfred Binet and follow a different path. Although he is known in the English-speaking world almost solely for his intelligence test, it was Binet who established experimental psychology in France. In 1890 he published in the *Revue philosophique* three important, but little-known, papers describing his pioneering efforts in psychological experimentation with his two little daughters, Madeleine and Alice.

From the time they were babies, the two sisters had very different styles of learning. When Madeleine, the older, was beginning to walk, she wouldn't let go of a chair she was holding onto until she spotted another support close by. Very serious, she took the few steps from one to the other in silence, paying strict attention to the movements of her legs. She learned to walk at twelve months.

Alice was ebullient, giddy, and laughing. She would stand for a few minutes, then impulsively stagger a few steps in any direction and fall down. She would just as soon go into an empty part of the room as toward a piece of furniture—she never anticipated where her course would lead. Although she was stronger than her sister, she didn't learn to walk until she was fifteen months old.

Madeleine always got on with the business at hand, whether it was walking, sleeping, or eating. From an early age she took her meals with her parents. Alice was so easily distracted by what she saw and heard at the table she would forget to eat— she had to have her meals alone.

It took a lot of patience to do experiments with Alice because her attention wandered. With Madeleine it was much easier. Here are two that Binet tried with her:

When she was a year and nine months old, he showed her a dozen pencil sketches of familiar objects— mere outline drawings, with no color and no perspective. She recognized a hat, a bottle, a glass, a table, a bowl, a chair, and an umbrella. The bowl was drawn with a cloud of steam over it— she said it was full of hot milk. But she didn't recognize at all the sketches of a mouth, a nose, a finger, and an ear. Binet repeated the experiment about three years later. Same results. Why? Binet thought it was because she had not yet developed the power to analyze, as adults do. We can take a picture apart and recognize parts of it separately. Madeleine had only seen noses and mouths as parts of a whole face. Seen in isolation, she didn't know what they were.

When she was four years old, he did an experiment with numbers. First, Binet carefully established the fact that she could only count to three. She knew the difference between two beans and three beans and could count them correctly, but if he put a fourth bean in the pile she was apt to say there were six or twelve or any number that popped into her head. This point is important because the aim of his experiment was to see if a child could perceive numbers without knowing how to count.

First he laid out two groups of round white counters— eighteen in one group, sixteen in the other, all spread out irregularly. Which group had more? Madeleine said,

"There," pointing to the eighteen counters. "There are more of them there." He changed the position of the groups and tried her again. Sometimes the big group was on the left, sometimes on the right, but it made no difference. She was right every time.

Then he replaced the eighteen white counters with eighteen much smaller green counters. Which group had more—the one with sixteen big white counters or eighteen little green counters? She was wrong on every trial. Binet surmised that she judged by the total space that the counters occupied. He took three of the small green counters and two of the big white counters and explained the difference to her. She understood and said there was a larger number of green ones, but the white ones were bigger.

He made some trials with groups of four and three to see if she really understood. She did, for these small numbers. But when he went to large groups of eighteen and fourteen, she was wrong again. His first conclusion was that Madeleine perceived a large group as a solid entity.

To fix the limits of the small groups that she could perceive as separate counters, he did trials starting with two green counters and one white counter and gradually increased the numbers to see how far she could go. She could compare numbers correctly up to five, but no higher. Binet's second conclusion was that her instinctive enumeration, however limited, was nevertheless greater than her counting ability, which only went to three.

Binet was convinced that observation of an individual's behavior in attempting a set task provides the best information about his intellectual performance. He said, "There is nothing much to be gained by turning the pages of authors who work apart from observation and experimentation." He continued his work with his daughters until they were in their teens and in 1903

published what many consider his best book, *L'étude
expérimentale de l'intelligence*, giving an account of his
experiments with them.

In the earlier papers Binet never used the words "my
daughters" but employed such expressions as "the two
little sisters who are, so to speak, constantly before my
eyes." In the book he attempted to disguise their
identity by calling them Marguerite and Armande.
(Possibly to save his teen-agers embarrassment?)

A number of these experiments are about the part
that images play in thought. Binet would say a word, and
one of his daughters would describe the image, if any,
that formed in her mind. Armande often complained that
she had to fight against distractions. Binet didn't go so
far as to say that she thought of one thing and visualized
another, but he did say that she was often like someone
who fires at a target and strikes to one side. For instance, when he said "elephant," she pictured the
platform in the zoo where children climbed on the
elephant, but there was no elephant. When he said
"cutlet," she saw the street and the red wall of the
butcher shop. No cutlet. He said, "A blast of wind carried
off the roof of the house." She saw a house, only it was
the railing, not the roof that was blown away. She had
these misses one time out of four. Binet accounted for it
by the fact that her sensory images came very rapidly
and she had little control over them. With Marguerite,
who was much better at directing the image, such in-
cidents were rare.

Sometimes he sprang his questions on them without
warning. In the middle of an ordinary conversation, or of
a different experiment, he would suddenly say, "Did you
have an image, and what was it?" Armande frequently
had none, Marguerite usually did, although it was
customarily of only part of the sentence. For instance,
when he said, "Departure in fifteen days for S— — —!"
methodical Marguerite pictured a sort of calendar.

Binet died in 1911, when he was only fifty-four. Eight years later young Jean Piaget arrived in Paris to study at the Sorbonne. He had previously earned degrees in natural science in his native Switzerland, with a doctoral thesis on mollusks. But his interests had turned to psychology and he had already done work at two laboratories and a psychiatric clinic in Zurich.

He attended some courses at the Sorbonne, but he was really looking for an experimental laboratory that he could use. He writes in his autobiography, "I had an extraordinary piece of luck. I was recommended to Dr. Simon who was then living in Rouen, but who had at his disposal Binet's laboratory at the grade school of the Rue de la Grange-aux-Belles in Paris. The laboratory was not being used because Simon had no classes in Paris at this time."

Simon offered the laboratory to Piaget and suggested that he use it to standardize Burt's reasoning tests on Parisian children (Cyril Burt, the English psychologist whose name keeps cropping up). Here is an example from Burt's test for ten-year-olds:

There are four roads here:
I have come from the South and want to go to Melton.
The road to the right leads somewhere else.
Straight ahead it leads only to a farm.
In which direction is Melton—North, South, East, or West?

Piaget undertook the standardization of the tests without much enthusiasm, but he says, "My mood soon changed; there I was, my own master, with a whole school at my disposition—unhoped-for working conditions." What fascinated him was not a statistical tabulation of right and wrong answers, but the children's reasoning processes that led them to give their answers, especially their wrong answers. What lay behind them? By what private logic did children reach conclusions perfectly reasonable to them but illogical to us?

To find out, he started using a technique much like that of a psychiatric examination—free conversation coupled with a verbatim record of everything the child said. In his autobiography he said, "Without Dr. Simon being quite aware of what I was doing, I continued for about two years to analyze the verbal reasoning of normal children by presenting them with various questions and exposing them to tasks involving simple concrete relations of cause and effect. . . . At last I had found my field of research."

Piaget wrote three articles reporting his results. The third brought him the offer of a position at the Institut J. J. Rousseau in Geneva, which he took, intending to stay for only a few years. But the institute became affiliated with the University of Geneva, and Piaget's "few years" stretched to fifty, until his recent retirement at the age of seventy-five.

During that time he has done a prodigious amount of research and has been a prolific writer, producing over thirty books and hundreds of articles. (He describes himself as "fundamentally a worrier whom only work can relieve.") His original aim of discovering what he called "the embryology of intelligence" led to the formulation of an original and brilliant theory of the stage-by-stage development of a child's mind.

Piaget himself was interested in studying intelligence, not in measuring it, and he ignored practically the whole business of IQ testing. However, his theory that a child's intelligence develops in sequential stages, each marked by characteristic and identifiable ways of thinking, would seem to lend itself to the construction of a scale for measuring mental maturity. There are now going on several major efforts by others to construct such a scale (see following chapters). These represent a departure from conventional IQ tests and are of great interest for the future. Whether you agree with Piaget's theory or not, it is important to know something of its rudiments in order to understand these new trends.

Like Binet, Piaget did many experiments with his own children—two daughters, Jacqueline and Lucienne, and a son, Laurent. He kept meticulously detailed records of what they did, records that are a gold mine of information about a baby's mental development.

For example, Jacqueline, his oldest and a good-natured child, was sitting on her bed playing with a celluloid duck on top of her quilt. She reached for it, but the duck slid down under the covers and was hidden by a fold of the sheet. As soon as it disappeared from sight she drew back her hand—it didn't occur to her to look under the sheet. Three times Piaget put the duck near her hand and when she tried to grab it covered it with the sheet while she watched. Each time she immediately gave up the minute the duck disappeared from view. He even took her hand and had her feel the duck through the sheet: Still she didn't lift the cover to look for it.

Jacqueline, who was seven months and twenty-eight days old at the time, had not yet developed the concept of the permanence of an object. Piaget says that the infant's world consists of shifting and unsubstantial tableaux that appear and then dissolve. The knowledge that an object exists independently, even when it is hidden from sight, is a milestone in a baby's mental growth.

Once they reach this milestone, the next question is Do they know where the object goes when it disappears? To find out, Piaget seated his son, Laurent (nine months and seventeen days old), on a sofa between a coverlet on one side and a wool garment on the other. He hid his watch under the coverlet while Laurent looked on attentively. The baby lifted the coverlet, saw part of the watch, and grabbed it. Piaget repeated the experiment:

Same thing. Then he hid the watch on the other side
under the wool garment, but Laurent hunted for it in the
same place where he had successfully found it before,
although he had plainly seen his father hide it elsewhere.

By the time Laurent was eleven months and twenty-
two days old, he had reached the next developmental
step. When Piaget seated him between two cushions and
hid the watch alternately under first one cushion and
then the other, Laurent always looked for it under the
cushion where it had just disappeared. He couldn't be
fooled.

Another series of experiments that Piaget did with his
children concerned the relationship of cause and effect.
His babies soon learned that by pulling a cord attached
to the hood of their bassinet they could shake the rattles
that were suspended there. But when Piaget untied the
string and attached the rattles to a pole two yards away,
they still pulled the cord on the bassinet to try to make
the rattles shake. The only cause the baby knows is his
own action. He doesn't realize that there has to be a
physical connection between the cord and the rattles.

The same thing was apparent in other situations.
When Laurent was seven months and twenty-nine days
old, Piaget put a box out of his reach on a rug. Laurent
succeeded one time in four in pulling the rug toward him
to get the box. Yet when Piaget held the box in the air
above the rug, Laurent still pulled the rug toward him to
try to get the box. Only later, when he was ten months
and sixteen days old, did Laurent discover that there
had to be contact between the rug and the desired object.

These observations and many more Piaget organized
into what he called the Sensory-Motor Period, covering
about the first two years of a child's life. During this time
the baby goes through a decentering process, starting
from an amorphous world with himself at the center and
ending with the construction of a permanent universe.

Here is a rough outline of the stages of this period:

## Sensory-Motor
### (Level of Direct Action upon Reality)
### 0 to eighteen months or two years

1. (0 to one month)
   Reflex.

2. (one to four months)
   First habits.

3. (four to eight months)
   Only cause he knows is in his own action (magical).
   Pulls cord to move rattles even if unattached and two yards away.

PERMANENCE OF OBJECT (eight or nine months)

4. (eight to twelve months)
   Can find object hidden at A, but if it is then hidden at B, he looks at A again.
   Can use means to reach an end, but no *new* means.

5. (twelve to eighteen months)
   Can find object wherever he sees it hidden. Will not pull rug or string unless object is in contact with it.
   Physical groping produces *new* means, by accident.

6. (eighteen months and on)
   Insight.
   Can figure out means first, then use it.
   Can infer to find object doubly hidden (under pillow behind screen, for example).

But just when the child has successfully gone through this decentering process, a new factor enters the picture. He learns to talk. Words are symbols that stand for physical objects and actions. If you say "car" and he knows what you mean even though no car is present, he has reached the level of representation.

The whole decentering process begins again at this new level, and this time it is much more difficult. There are many obstacles in the way. For one thing, decentering is harder to do on the level of mental representation than on the level of action. For another, the child's universe is now a social one containing other persons who have their own views—not merely people-as-objects, as they were in the Sensory-Motor Period.

Little children are completely enmeshed in their own viewpoints, even in a physical sense. For example, they are not aware that to somebody on the other side of the room a table looks different from the way it looks to them. It is not easy to develop the understanding that there are many possible perspectives of which theirs is but one.

They can't take another's viewpoint figuratively speaking, either. For instance, they make up their own names for things—one little boy I know said "hairpoo" for "shampoo"—and just assume that everybody else knows what the word means. (That one is pretty plain, but sometimes they aren't!) They talk *at* another person, rather than to him. They can't mentally put themselves in the listener's place and choose words that will convey their meaning to him.

This second decentering process lasts from the time the child is one and a half or two until about the age of twelve. Most of Piaget's experiments with children in this period were done at the Maison des Petits, a kindergarten connected with the Institut J. J. Rousseau, or with pupils in the Geneva school system in the same way that he had previously worked with pupils in Binet's laboratory at the grade school of the Rue de la Grange-aux-Belles in Paris.

Just as the concept of the permanent object comes at the middle of the Sensory-Motor Period, a kindred concept begins to develop about halfway through this long second period. Piaget calls it conservation. To understand what he means by the term, erase from your mind everything you know about quantity and the words we use to describe it—large, small, many, few, inches, feet, counting, dozens, pints, gallons, etc. Go back mentally, back as far as you can, and try to think like a child. What is the most fundamental of all ideas about quantity? It is the fact that the basic amount of something doesn't change merely because its appearance is altered.

Little children don't know this. Instead of the constants we see, they live in a world in flux, with quantity and number continually enlarging and diminishing. For example, here is an experiment on conservation of number done with a little boy named Jon, who was four years and five months old. Piaget laid out in a row six red counters equally spaced. Then he showed Jon a box of blue counters and asked him to take out as many as there were on the table. At first Jon put seven in his row, pushed close together so that the end points coincided with Piaget's. He judged the number by the space occupied, disregarding the gaps between the objects. (Note that this is remarkably similar to the conclusion that Binet had drawn from his experiment with his four-year-old daughter Madeleine when he wrote that she was judging number by the total space that the counters occupied.)

Jon corrected himself and got the right number by laying a blue counter opposite each red one. When Piaget asked, "Are they the same?" Jon said, "Yes." Then Piaget spread Jon's row out and repeated his question. Jon said, "No."

"Has one of us got more?"

"Me."

"Make it so you have the same number as I have."

Jon moved his counters closer together.

"Are they the same?"

"Yes."

"Why?"

"Because I pushed mine together."

Six objects spread out seemed to him to be more than six objects clustered close together. He did not understand that sixness is preserved through all changes in arrangement. In other words, he was not yet a conserver of number.

I tried this same experiment with a group of first-graders, using a row of eight poker chips. One little boy had a slight speech impediment, a sort of lisp, that made him seem babyish, but his reasoning was right on target. When I asked him if we both had the same number or if one of us had more, he looked at me as if I had lost my mind. "They were like thith," he said, pointing to the space opposite mine where his chips had been. "I mean, you didn't take one *out*, so they've got to be the thame."

Another experimenter and I were doing the testing simultaneously in different corners of the room. Without saying anything to anybody, one boy went to both of us. No one noticed until after we had finished and were counting up the number of conservers. There was Peter's name on both our lists.

When his teacher asked him about it the next day, he readily admitted that he knew he wasn't supposed to be tested twice. "I just wanted to see what the other lady had," he said. What she had were exactly the same things I did, except her poker chips were blue and white and mine were red and white.

Here is an abbreviated version of an experiment Piaget did on the conservation of liquids with a little girl named Clairette, who was four. Piaget said, "Have you got a friend?"

"Yes, Odette."

"Look, we're giving you, Clairette, a glass of orangeade, and we're giving Odette a glass of lemonade. Has one of you more to drink than the other?"

"The same."

Piaget poured Clairette's orangeade into a tall, narrow glass, where the level naturally reached much higher, and repeated the question. Clairette said, "I've got more."

"Why?"

"We poured it into that glass." She pointed to the level.

"But were they the same before?"

"Yes."

"And now?"

"I've got more."

By the time they were eight, most of the children reasoned as we would, that the amount of orangeade stayed the same in spite of the way it looked in the narrow glass.

We tried the experiment on conservation of liquids with the same group of first-graders that we had tested for conservation of number. Instead of orangeade and lemonade we used water tinted with red and green food coloring. What struck me was the children's absolute certainty. The nonconservers' attitude was, "Of course there's more. Look," and they pointed to the higher level in the tall glass. The conservers were surprised that we asked them such a silly question—naturally the amount was the same. A few were in a transitional period between the two extremes. One boy wavered, then said, "Pour it back in the first glass and let me see it again."

According to Piaget, somewhere between the ages of four and eight (the exact time varying from child to child) children develop the understanding that enables them to conserve quantity—not overnight, but through a period of gradual change. And not at the same time for all kinds of things. A child might know that the amount stayed the same if colored beads were poured from one glass to another but not if liquids were poured. He might conserve quantity when a ball of clay was patted into a different shape but not conserve the length of a stick if it was moved to a different position. Last of all come the conservation of weight, usually at around nine or ten years, and conservation of volume, at about twelve years of age.

I saw for myself an example of the difficulty that children have with the conservation of volume in a seventh-grade science class in America. The teacher was trying to give the pupils an idea of how much 1,000 cubic centimenters is. He set out a graduate—a very tall, thin cylinder plainly marked *1,000 cc's*—and filled it with water. Then he put out a low, wide beaker, also marked *1,000 cc's*, and said, "I'm going to pour all the water out of the graduate into the beaker."

The children said, "You can't." "It won't hold it." "The water'll go all over the place."

When he did, they were skeptical. "You poured some of it up your sleeve."

He said, "Look, I'll do it with my jacket off," and did so. Even though the water filled the beaker just to the brim, they still didn't believe it. They didn't even believe it when they poured it themselves. The visual impact of that tall, tall column of water in the graduate was so strong that logic meant nothing. To paraphrase a colleague of Piaget's, it was the eyes of the body and not those of the mind that prevailed.

Piaget divides this long second decentering process into two parts—the Preoperational Period, covering the ages between two and about six or seven, and the Period of Concrete Operations, which lasts until about eleven or twelve. The "operations" that the names refer to are complex mental acts that the older children can do but the younger ones can't.

One of these is classification—a logical process that underlies all types of analytical thinking. At first glance this seems simple enough. Children learn at an early age to put all the red blocks in one pile and all the blue ones in another. But when one class includes another, it proves too complicated.

For example, here is an experiment that Piaget did with a little girl named Ric, who was five years eleven months old. He showed her a picture of some flowers, most of them poppies but a few bluebells. "Look at these poppies and these bluebells. If I take all the flowers, or if I take the poppies, which will be the biggest bunch?"

"The bunch of poppies because there are more."

"Show me the poppies." She pointed correctly. "Show me the flowers." She pointed to the whole picture. "Then which bunch will be bigger, the one with the flowers or the one with the poppies?"

"The one with the poppies."

This is not an accidental mistake; her answers are typical of children in the Preoperational Period. They can't think of the whole and its parts at the same time. To them, the whole is destroyed when it is split into parts. Ric understood very well that some were poppies, some were bluebells, and that they were all flowers. But she couldn't reason about the whole (flowers) and a part (poppies) at the same time. When she thought about one she forgot the other. Asked to compare the poppies with something, since to her the whole was gone, she compared them to the only thing left—the bluebells. Obviously, there were more poppies. Classification is not mastered until the concept of class inclusion is mastered.

A second operation involves the relationship among objects—for example, the ability to arrange a group of things in order according to some characteristic, such as

size. The key to making a series lies in the knowledge
that if Pencil A is longer than Pencil B, and Pencil B is
longer than Pencil C, then Pencil A is longer than Pencil
C. Little children don't understand this. They have to
physically compare the two pencils to see which is
longer.

It's the same with any relationship, not just size.
Whether it's "redder than," "bumpier than," "colder
than," or whatever, they can correctly compare A and B,
and also B and C, but they can't put the two facts
together. Until they develop this logical concept,
arranging a complete series is beyond them; they
construct only disconnected fragments.

Here are some of the highlights of the decentering
process at the level of representation:

### Level of Representation

I. Preoperational Period (two to six or seven years
old)

Representation of the universe shows precausality
— for example, "Snow is for children to play in."

Doesn't differentiate between internal and external
world.

Doesn't differentiate between his own viewpoint
and that of others, either literally or figuratively.

Doesn't grasp the notion of chance.

Can't deduce that if A is larger than B, and B larger
than C, then A is larger than C. Must compare A
and C physically.

BEGINNING OF CONSERVATION (seven or
eight)

II. Period of Concrete Operations (seven or eight to
eleven or twelve) (Relates directly to objects, but
not verbally stated hypotheses.)

Has mastered classification.

Has mastered seriation— doesn't have to compare A and C physically to deduce relation, provided A and C are concrete objects. Verbal statements, such as "Mary is older than John and John is older than Sue" tell him nothing about Mary and Sue's comparative ages.

Differentiates between his own viewpoint and that of others.

Is a conserver of number, substance, length, surface, weight, etc.

Grasps the notion of chance.

At this point, once again a new factor comes into play requiring a third and final decentering process that lasts to about the age of fourteen or fifteen. This new factor is that the content of the child's thought changes. He is no longer restricted to thinking about the concrete but can now think about anything. He can think about his previous thoughts, or about abstractions, or about unproven hypotheses that may or may not be true— it doesn't matter, because he can disconnect his thought from objects.

Piaget calls this the period of Formal Operations, since it is the form, not the content, of the child's thinking that is characteristic. Presented with a problem, he considers all the possibilities, and from among these "might be's" he systematically works toward a solution.

In a typical experiment, Piaget put out five bottles filled with colorless, odorless liquids. Without letting the child see how he did it, Piaget mixed some of the liquids and produced a yellow color. Then he gave the child a medicine dropper and some glasses and asked him to make the yellow color for himself, using the liquids in the five bottles any way he wanted to.

Actually it was the mixture of liquids A, C, and E that worked. D was a bleach that prevented the color from forming, and B was plain water. The children, of course, didn't know this in advance. The younger ones mixed the liquids haphazardly. But a thirteen-year-old boy named Cha said, "You have to try with all the bottles. I'll begin with the one at the end." He tried all possible combinations of pairs. When none of these worked, he started combining the liquids three at a time and discovered not only that the mixture of A, C, and E worked but also that no other mixture of three did. Piaget said, "Then what is there in B and D?" Cha said, "B is certainly water since it doesn't act on the liquids. D isn't water; it's something harmful."

At this stage, a child can combine verbal propositions or ideas the same way that he can combine objects. The combination of propositions according to certain rules is the heart of the formal subject of logic, and Piaget relies very heavily on what is now called symbolic logic to explain the reasoning of the child in the period of Formal Operations. (Not that the child has to know the rules of logic, any more than a singer has to know the formal rules of harmony.)

Piaget believes that symbolic logic explains a core system that the child develops for putting together all the operations that he could handle earlier only in piecemeal fashion. For example, in the realm of thought for every action there exists another action that undoes it. This reversibility is of two kinds. On the physical level, shortening can be negated by lengthening or it can be compensated for by widening. In the preceding period, the child understands each of these two kinds of reversibility separately but he has no overall system for combining the two. Without such a system he can't understand such things as proportion, probability, and double reference (a snail crawling on a board that is itself moving in a different direction). The same two kinds of reversibility, negation and compensation, hold at the abstract level and are an integral part of symbolic logic.

Here are some features of this final decentering process:

Formal Operations (Level of Thought)
(eleven or twelve to fourteen or fifteen years of age)

Can conceive, in advance, all possible combinations
of objects.
Can combine verbal propositions or ideas in the
same way.
Can understand proportion, probability, and double
systems of reference.
Can solve a problem by varying one factor at a time,
holding everything else constant.
Can think about the hypothetical.

Conventional IQ tests don't fit Piaget's theory because they are essentially additive, like beads on a string. The question they attempt to answer is How long is your string? True, there is some variety among the beads, although far too many are made of the basic material of verbal ability. But one bead does not depend on another. Piaget's "embryology of intelligence" is more like the developing fetus— one stage of growth must precede the next.

# Chapter 7
## A New Kind of Mental Scale
## Based on Piaget

Of all the criticisms that have been hurled at IQ tests, the most deep-rooted is that they are not based on any theory of mental development. They are compiled of disconnected items, devised by asking, "What can a six-year-old child do?" or "What can a high school senior do?" In a word, they are artificial, being built from the outside in.

A natural scale, on the other hand, would be built from the inside out by starting with the stages of mental development and looking for questions to identify each. Age would be the last factor considered, not the first.

A major effort to construct such a natural scale is taking place at the University of Montreal's Institute of Psychology under the direction of Adrien Pinard, a psychologist who is also a follower of Piaget. In explaining their purposes, he says, "Can one say that the usual intelligence scales truly interpret a natural development? In real evolution, the attainment of a given level generally presupposes the mastery of the preceding level. . . . It is well known that in an age scale, such as Terman's for example, this condition is not met."

Conventional tests are a hodgepodge of items, a

collection of fragments. What Pinard and his group are seeking is a test that would identify a larva-chrysalis-butterfly type of progression. They do not intend a numerical IQ-like evaluation at all but are aiming for an entirely new kind of test for children. By employing problems similar to Piaget's, they would describe the point a child had reached in developing each of certain basic mental concepts, using Piaget's theory as an index.

Their first step was to investigate to what extent the stages that he had found in the children of Geneva would appear in another population—in this case, the French-Canadian children of Montreal. If it turned out that the same stages were present, the next step—selecting the problems that most clearly indicate each level of mental evolution and combining them into a workable test— would naturally follow.

There have been hundreds of other validation studies of Piaget's work conducted in a great many different places—England, France, the United States, and Norway, to name a few. In general, they found the same sequence of stages of mental development as Piaget, although the children did not fit quite so neatly into the patterns. Especially, there was more variation of age than he had said.

The tendency in these studies has been to specialize in certain areas of Piaget's work, with his experiments on conservation of number and quantity perhaps the most popular. Other experiments—for instance, those on children's concepts of time and speed—have been repeated very little.

Some have been done in unusual and exotic places. An experimenter in Aden tested Arab, Indian, and Somali children, phrasing the questions in Arabic, the language they used in school. She reported that many of them gave answers in Arabic that were almost word for word the same thing Piaget's Swiss children had said in French.

Not every experimenter got quite so neat a fit. A Harvard graduate student sat in a thatched hut in a village compound in the African bush, poured the water, and asked the familiar question, "Do the glasses have equal water or does one have more?" She found that the children's belief in witchcraft intervened: They thought the tall glass had more because the experimenter possessed magical powers and she had done the pouring. When she let the children pour the water themselves, they reasoned like children in other parts of the world.

Aside from witchcraft, many validation studies have showed that changing the way the experiment is set up makes a difference. For instance, if the problem is presented so that the concept is less dependent on verbal understanding, children often exhibited it at a younger age.

But all this work has been done under such varying conditions that the results cannot be compared accurately, and much of it has been fragmentary in scope. Therefore it could not serve as the basis for a standardized test.

The Montreal group considered the whole sweep of Piaget's research on mental development, chose twenty-five of his principal experiments, and systematically set out to repeat them under uniform conditions. They did so in the manner that scientific research is now conducted, with all the attendant statistical safeguards.

Piaget gave little background information on his subjects beyond their ages and occasional comments like "Subject very precocious." He rarely told how many children he examined, and his method of selecting them doesn't seem to have been made according to any very strict procedures.

On the other hand, the Montreal group used all the orthodox methods to secure a true cross section of the child population. They chose 700 children, 50 at each age level from two years old to twelve. Because intellectual growth is faster in the early years, the age interval was six months for those under five and twelve months for the rest. Every level was divided half and half between boys and girls. The occupations of their parents conformed to the percentages given in the census data.

School-age children were distributed according to academic level— precocious, normal, or retarded— in the proportions given in the figures of the School Commission. Since this information was not available for preschoolers, they were divided among families with one child, families with two children, and families with three or more, in accordance with the census data.

All children were tested as near their birthdays as possible. For six-year-olds, this posed a problem. As in the United States, Canadian children begin the first grade of school when they are six, but their exact age depends on the relation between their birthday and the beginning of the school term. Some are six many months before the opening of school, some do not have their sixth birthdays until they are already in school. For statistical purposes, Pinard classed all six-year-olds as preschoolers.

The average amount of time spent with each child was ten hours, split into anywhere from four to eight sessions according to his age. Schoolchildren were tested at school in an isolated room during school hours. Preschoolers were tested at home. Whenever possible, the examiner asked to be left alone with the child, but for very young or shy ones, the mother often stayed in the room (and the examiner couldn't have managed if she hadn't).

Though faced with a wide variety of home situations, efforts were made to keep the testing conditions reasonably uniform. For instance, the directions for a test that used ten toy houses and ten toy pine trees, all graduated in size, throws in this hint: "If the table is too small to allow the alignment of all the houses leaving one-half inch between each, have this test on the floor."

The examiners were graduate psychology students who before fanning out for their assignments had received special training in the difficult art of questioning children. Where Piaget varied his questions from child to child, the Montreal researchers were provided with guidelines of what and what not to say and do. In the example above, which basically was a test of the child's ability to arrange the toy houses into a series according to size, to do the same with the pine trees, and then match them up, there are such warnings as these:*

> . . . do not say, for example, to put the biggest tree with the biggest house. . . .
>
> If the child proposes a series which contains one or several errors, note first his response (order and arrangement of the elements) and continue to question him.
>
> Note the answer of the child each time and also indicate his way of proceeding: if he tries to count, to follow with his fingers, etc. . . .
>
> Let him redo the series of the trees and/or the houses if he wants to, but never suggest he do so.

All in all, their method was about midway between Piaget's free questioning and the objective technique of traditional tests.

The Montreal pilot study is unique in that for the most part all twenty-five tests were given to the same group of children. There was some variation, depending on the youngest children's ability to deal with the experiment—one test might be taken by all those from two and a half to twelve years old, another by those from two to ten. That children of such a wide age range could take the same test is explained by the fact that they respond to

---

*For this and other unpublished tests I am indebted to Professor Pinard, who permitted me to see them (in French).

the same questions in different ways, according to their stage of mental development.

Here, for example, is a test on the concept of space that children from three to twelve years old took. Contrary to what we adults might think, space is an intellectual construction, built up step by step from primitive notions of neighborhood "by the table," "near the bed," without taking into account the distances between objects, to the more sophisticated ideas of right-left, before-behind, and their coordination.

For the test, the examiner lays out side by side two identical pictures made of cardboard. A road and a railroad track intersecting it are drawn flat on each, as in a bird's-eye view. Explaining that one picture is his and one is the child's, he says, "Now, we are going to put houses on our pictures. We will put the houses the same way on both pictures. See, here I am putting a red house. Now you should put a red house on your picture. There should be one at the same place so that the two pictures will be just alike."

Proceeding in the same way, they add a yellow house to each picture and then a cluster of three smaller houses, all the same size but different colors, down near the corner of each board. To play the game (take the test), the examiner and the child each has a little clay man, and every time the examiner places his man in a certain spot on his board, the child is to do the same on his.

For example, the examiner puts his doll on the roof of the red house and says something like, "See, I am putting my man here. You do the same thing; put your man in the same place in your picture so he will be just like mine." The examiner places his doll in twelve different positions, each time telling the child to put his man "at exactly the same place" but never giving any verbal hints like "near the railroad tracks" or "in front of the yellow house."

For the second part of the test, one board is reversed so that it is upside down in relation to the other. Again the examiner, who is sitting on the opposite side of the table from the child, puts his doll in the same twelve positions with the same instructions. This is much harder than the first time, requiring a double reversal— both of right-left and before-behind—because the child has to be able to visualize the scene from the point of view of the examiner, who is facing him.

The records of the children's answers to this test, as on all the other tests, were evaluated by Pinard and another professor of psychology at the institute, Monique Laurendeau, working together, and then reviewed by a third scorer independently. The criterion in scoring was the quality of reasoning displayed, not the number of correct responses given within a timed interval to a lot of separate items. Each answer is important not for itself but as part of a whole showing a trend toward a certain kind of thinking.

On this test, some of the positions that the little man was put in were easy to spot because of neighboring cues—he was right by the red house, or he was on the road. Other positions were harder because they were out in the open and the child had to coordinate several factors to locate the man correctly.

The reversal of the board was basically meant to differentiate between the level of mental development characteristic of Piaget's Preoperational Period and his Concrete Operational Period. Those children who could do most of the first part of the test but not the second were still tied to their own point of view and were unaware that from the opposite side of the board things looked different. Children who could successfully handle the second part of the test had decentered their concept of space and could visualize the scene from another person's viewpoint.

The scorers' analysis of the answers of the 600 children who took this test resulted in these stages:

Stage 0—Refusal or incomprehension of the instructions:

Only eight children fell in this group. Some tried one or two problems and then flatly refused to go on. Others were more docile but showed that they didn't understand in the least, giving reasons like, "It's prettier here," and "I like that one better." Or they put their little man in the same place every time, paying no attention to where the examiner put his—in other words, they were just playing with the material.

Stage 1—Child understands and likes to play the game but considers only such things as neighborhood. He is unable to consider distances or directions or even to coordinate several neighborhoods. For instance, he puts his man up against the red house instead of midway between the red house and the road. Many errors are caused by the child's merely imitating the examiner's gesture. For instance, if the examiner makes a long movement passing over the yellow house, the child does the same, without considering where the doll will land.

Stage 2—Child succeeds with first part of the test, when the two boards are placed alike, but in the second half he still places his man in the same relation to his own body, as if the board had not been turned at all. For instance, he places his doll on the road all right, but it is on the opposite end of the road from where it should be. His concept of space is still entirely egocentric. This stage is divided into two substages, according to whether the child succeeds with only the easier positions of the first part of the test or whether he can do all the first part of the test.

Stage 3—Child can solve problems when the board is reversed. He can visualize the scene from a viewpoint other than his own. This decentration comes slowly and is divided into two substages. In the first he can reverse either the left-right direction or the before-behind direction but not both at once. He can't coordinate the two. In the second substage, he can achieve the double reversal and can solve most problems in both sections of the test.

Pinard has another test on the concept of space in which the same little clay man is placed at successively different spots on a model of a landscape with three mountains. They pretend he is a photographer. What would the picture he takes here look like? The child is shown five cards to choose from for each position.

To get the feel of the test and some firsthand observation of the way children react to it, I made a model according to Pinard's specifications and, in a purely informal way, tried two of the positions with 50 eighth-graders and 50 sixth-graders. It was too easy for the eighth-graders, who were thirteen or fourteen years old. (Remember that the oldest children in Pinard's group were twelve.)

Most of them could do it readily, but I got a few interesting answers. One girl chose a mirror image of the right picture—something that the photographer could have seen only if he had been in a car driving away from the mountains and looking in the rearview mirror. When I pointed this out to her, she said, "My parents think I see things backward."

The test was well suited for the sixth-graders, most of whom were eleven or twelve years old. About half of them could do the harder position and about three-fourths the easier position of the toy photographer.

Another group of tests in the Montreal research are on the concept of conservation, an important (and hotly debated) part of Piaget's theory. Of the three different experiments in this area that they chose to replicate, the one on the conservation of substance using two balls of clay is probably the best known of all Piaget's experiments on any subject. Pinard's group didn't repeat merely the very familiar part but carried it all the way through into the less publicized portion on conservation of weight and volume using those same two balls.

Their materials were a square glass jar, a grease pencil, scales of the balance type, and two little balls of plasticine two inches in diameter. The examiner shows the balls to the child and asks, "Is there the same amount of dough in the two?" If he says no, the examiner changes them by adding or subtracting plasticine until the child is convinced they are the same.

Then he asks, "Are the two equally heavy?" If the child says no, the examiner puts them on the scales to show him that they balance. To be sure that the child understands the meaning of balanced scales, he makes use of other objects that are obviously heftier or lighter and points out that it is only when the two are the same weight that the two sides of the scales are straight across.

To establish equality of volume, the examiner puts some water in the glass jar and says, "I am making a line with my pencil just at the place where the water reaches." Then he puts one of the balls in the jar and marks the new level, saying something like, "See, the water has risen. When we put things in the water, then the water rises. Do you understand? The water has risen just to here, so I am making another line with my pencil so I can remember how high the water reached."

He takes the first ball out of the water and puts the second one in, saying, "See, the water has risen to the same place that it did before. The two balls take up the same amount of room because the water rose to the same height both times."

All this preliminary is required because it is absolutely necessary that the child believe that the two balls are equal in substance, in weight, and in volume before the experiment proper can begin.

In problem one, the examiner takes one ball, rolls it out and joins the two ends to form a ring, leaving the other ball in its original shape. He shows the child the ring and asks, "If I put it in the water, show me with your finger just how high the water will rise. . . . You are sure? . . . Why?" (Always "Why?"—it is the child's reasons that are illuminating, not the number of correct predictions, some of which might come by chance.)

Then he says, "If I put the ball and the ring on the scale, will one be heavier? . . . You are sure? . . . Why?"

"And now, tell me, does one have more dough in it than the other? Why?"

Piaget found that the younger children said the quantity of clay stayed the same when it was made into a different shape but that the weight and the volume changed. Those a few years older knew that the weight also stayed the same but thought the volume changed. Only when they reached the Period of Formal Operations did they think that the volume remained unaltered. He concluded that conservation of the properties of the clay balls developed in three sequential stages whose order was fixed—first global quantity, then weight, and finally volume.

If the results of the Montreal group's meticulous research using such a large number of children turn out to confirm Piaget's contention that this is a normal evolutionary order, then it does appear to be a promising tool for measuring intellectual development.

Another area of thought that the Montreal battery of tests explores concerns children's ideas about time, movement, and speed. Piaget first undertook these experiments at Einstein's request. Adults usually consider time as a primary concept and speed as something derived from the relation between time and distance. On the other hand, in Einstein's theory it is velocity that is the primary concept, and time is relative to it. Einstein wanted Piaget to investigate which concept, speed or time, children developed first. Piaget agreed and did enough research on the subject to fill two books: *Le développement de la notion de temps chez l'enfant* and *Les notions de mouvement et de vitesse chez l'enfant.*

He found that velocity did seem to be the more primitive notion and that it was not dependent on an idea of time. However, speed is not the same thing to children as it is to adults. Children derive their ideas about the speed of a moving object—say, a toy car—by seeing it pass another toy car and therefore judging it to be faster. And they have to actually see the car in the act of overtaking the other one. If tunnels were put over the roads that the toy cars were on, hiding the act of overtaking, they couldn't infer that one must have passed the other and therefore couldn't infer anything about the speeds.

The Montreal group repeated five of Piaget's experiments on these concepts. Here is a typical one on speed: The examiner lays out a semicircular board representing a racetrack with two toy autos on it connected on the underside by a wooden bar. By turning a crank he can make the bar move, like the spoke of a wheel.

He shows the whole apparatus to the child, saying, "I

can make the cars work so that they advance, both of them at the same time," and he works them a little, both forward and backward, over a small portion of the track.

He explains that the cars are going to have a race, and he points with his finger to the route that the outside car is going to follow near the edge of the semicircle and to the other car's route near the center. "Which one, do you think, is going to arrive first? Try to guess which of the two cars is going to win the race." If the child picks one, or if he says that they will arrive at the same time, the examiner asks him why he thinks so and notes verbatim all of his answers.

Then the examiner actually makes the cars go by turning the crank until they get to the end of the track. "Did they leave at the same time? . . . Did they arrive at the same time? . . . Then, tell me, is there one which went more quickly than the other? Is there one which hurried more than the other?"

Whichever way the child answers, the examiner, as usual, asks him why. If the child wants to see the race again, he repeats it as often as necessary. He even takes two pieces of string, measures each route, and lays the strings out straight side by side so that it is obvious that one route is longer than the other.

Piaget found that the younger children thought both cars traveled at the same speed because neither passed the other. Gradually they progress to a stage where, after watching the race, they change their minds and say that the outer auto goes faster, although at first they can't explain why.

Many of the rest of the experiments in the Montreal pilot study are on the central Piagetian operations of classification, relationship, and number. The test on arranging ten toy houses and ten toy pine trees in a series according to size (mentioned early in this chapter) is from this group.

Another of these tests is on children's ideas of

probability or chance. Piaget wrote only one book on this subject, and there have been few validation studies made of the experiments described in it. Briefly, he found that a child in the Preoperational Period doesn't comprehend that there is any such thing as chance or luck. If a tray with red beads at one end and white beads at the other is tilted back and forth so that the beads are gradually mixed, he believes that in the end they will all become unmixed again. A child in the Concrete Operational Period recognizes chance events when he sees them, but he lacks the intellectual equipment to handle them. Not until the Period of Formal Operations is the complete concept of probability established, because it depends on proportion.

The materials for the Montreal group's experiment are six black marbles, six white marbles, two miniature plates, and two cones that fit over the plates to form lids. The examiner sets out the two plates on a table, puts a few marbles in one, and shows the child how by putting a cone over them the marbles are hidden. Then he takes the whole collection of marbles, points out that some are black and some are white, and puts them away in a place where the child can't see them.

To play the game he says something like, "I am going to put some marbles in these two plates. Watch the marbles that I have put in each plate well, because I am going to hide them with the two cones." He puts two black marbles in one plate, two white marbles in the other plate, and covers them with the lids.

"If you want to get a black marble on the first try, without looking [under the lids], which plate will you choose? In which plate are you more sure of finding a black marble? . . . Why do you choose that plate?"

The examiner notes verbatim the child's answers and repeats the game using different combinations of marbles each time. The combinations range in difficulty from the very obvious one above to those where not only the relation of blacks to whites varies but the total number of marbles under each cone is different. Some impossibilities are included, as when neither plate contains any black marbles, as well as some dead certainties—only one marble in the plate and it is black. In some cases the collection of marbles in each plate is identical—say, two whites and one black in each.

All together they play the game twenty-four times. The exact combination of black and white marbles, the order in which the combinations are given, and even which go in the plate to the left and which in the plate to the right are specified each time. The examiner is told never to mention the number of marbles which are placed in each of the plates but merely to say something like, "Here I put that, and here I put that." If the child wants to prove that he is right by drawing out one marble from the plate that he chose, the examiner lets him do it and makes a note of his action and also what color he drew.

The enormity of the task of analyzing the results of all twenty-five tests is apparent. In some cases the number of children taking each test was 500, ranging in age from four to twelve, but for a specific test it could be anywhere from 400 to 700. Their answers were classified on the basis of quality of reasoning displayed—all the tests allowed for at least three levels of response and some as many as six.

The fact that hundreds of the same children took the whole battery allows an across-the-board comparison of a child's thinking on one test with his thinking on another, which should be very significant. It also increases the amount of statistical work to be done and the time it will take to do it.

The results announced so far do seem to confirm the existence of Piaget's stages, with minor variations. The Montreal children generally reached each developmental stage at a slightly later age than the children that Piaget used in his experiments. In most cases they were only a year or two older, with a few spectacular exceptions. Quite probably the difference in age can be accounted for by the fact that the French-Canadian children were systematically selected to represent the whole population, where Piaget's were not.

Another major effort to construct an intelligence test grounded on Piaget's theory is being carried out at the University of Geneva by Bärbel Inhelder and Vinh-Bang, both co-workers of Piaget's. They have selected about thirty Piagetian tasks and administered them to a large group of children from four to twelve years of age. Where Piaget did not give all his subjects the same task, or always present it in exactly the same way, they have attempted to standardize the procedures, making the testing conditions uniform.

Some of their tests are the same as Pinard's, and he and Vinh-Bang have compared notes by personal correspondence. For instance, in the test on space described earlier in the chapter, in Vinh-Bang's version the child not only has to put his clay man in the same position on the landscape as the examiner's but his man must appear to be looking in the same direction. Pinard's doll is purposely made without any modeling to indicate eyes, or even a face, so it doesn't matter which way he is turned, as long as he is placed at the right spot in relation to the houses, road, etc.

The parallel efforts of these two important groups of psychologists, both aimed at the same goal, would seem to increase the likelihood of the early construction of a new type of test for children. Because it gets at something deeper than present tests, it could be a tool for diagnosis, not merely for evaluation. Its usefulness in the schools would be enormous. Perhaps a first-grader is having trouble with math. Such a test would show whether or not he was a conserver yet. How can he understand anything about measurement as long as he thinks the size of the thing being measured keeps changing when it is moved from place to place? How can he understand addition and subtraction if he thinks the number of objects in a group keeps changing every time they are rearranged? The realization that they stay put is one of the greatest hurdles that child thought has to clear.

If arithmetic is imposed on a child before he develops the necessary concepts, sometimes he gets along by merely memorizing the rules, without understanding what he is doing. This works all right until about the fourth grade, when the accumulation of rules gets too ponderous and complex to handle. Then we have the case, familiar to every teacher, of the student who is good verbally, shows adequate reasoning ability, but is poor in math.

Usually he is convinced that he is just dumb in the subject, because on the type of IQ test commonly used in the schools, verbal and math scores are reported separately, and his math scores are low. Actually, his ability is usually at least as good as average. The trouble is that he got off on the wrong foot to start with and has avoided the subject as much as possible ever since (which is only natural).

As he progresses through school, the situation becomes worse. Since he didn't learn fourth-grade math, he can't do what comes in the fifth grade, therefore he has trouble with sixth grade, and so on. All this trauma could have been avoided if the cause had been spotted in the beginning.

Another trouble spot where such a test could track down the difficulty has to do with the ability to deal with abstractions. Suppose the test showed that a child was still in the stage of concrete operations; he couldn't be expected to handle topics that required abstract reasoning.

# Chapter 8
# A Broadened View
# of Intelligence

As the IQ cult has lost its grip on the public, a broader view of intelligence is emerging. Much of the current experimentation is on cognitive style, a shadowy area that lies between the old narrow IQ concept and personality.

Research on cognitive style coalesces around the way our minds process information—an intriguing subject. Most people are almost totally unaware that others are processing information in different ways from themselves. When they know this, it may give them a more accurate—and more reassuring—self-estimate.

One of the first experimenters in this area was David Witkin. He is a critic of conventional IQ tests because of their heavy emphasis on verbal skills. In an article in *Child Development* he said that their use tended to "route children through life" on the basis of verbal competence.

He added that "Children who show a deficit in the verbal area, whatever other cognitive strengths they may have . . . are therefore likely to be referred for special testing. Moreover, these children are particularly penalized on standard intelligence tests. . . . Thus, the verbally handicapped child is not only more likely to be referred for testing than children with other cognitive deficits but, when tested, is more likely to earn a low IQ, with the prospect of being classified as retarded."

Beginning at Brooklyn College in 1944 and later moving to the Downstate Medical Center of the State University of New York, Witkin and his associates established the existence of a mental faculty that he called field dependence. It concerns the ability to separate an object from its background when there are competing cues.

In his early experiments he used very elaborate equipment— a small room that could be tilted to the left or right and a chair that could also be tilted left or right. The subject sits in the tilted chair inside the tilted room and the experimenter moves the chair until the subject says he thinks he is sitting up straight.

The point is that we judge which way is up by two standards. One is the feeling within ourselves caused by the pull of gravity; the other is by the appearance of our surroundings— the walls, doors, corners, etc., of a room, if we are indoors. If these are tilted, as they were in Witkin's room, the two standards conflict. Which is dominant? Do you rely on the sensations from within, or do you align yourself to conform to the slanted room, as one child did who answered yes to the question, "Is this the way you sit when you eat your dinner?" when actually she was tilted at an angle of 35 degrees.

Anybody can straighten himself when he is blind-folded; the test comes from the conflict between the visual cues and the inward feeling. Those who are influenced by the slanted room Witkin called field dependent; those who aligned themselves nearly upright in spite of what they saw, he called field independent.

He then devised a simpler test for the same ability. The subject sits in a darkened room and looks at what appears to be a luminous frame for a picture, except that instead of a picture, there is a movable luminous rod inside it. Both are tilted. The experimenter moves the rod around until the subject says that he thinks it is upright. The people who line the rod up according to the slanted sides of the frame are the same people who are seduced by the slanting walls of the tilting room. Those who can straighten themselves up in the tilted chair can also adjust the rod so it is upright.

The ability improves with age, especially between the ages of eight and thirteen, then it levels off and even regresses slightly in the late teens. But for a given individual it is remarkably stable. Those at the top of their group when they are eight are usually still at the top of their group when they are sixteen.

Both of these tests correlate with the Embedded Figure Test, which is something like those newspaper puzzles showing a drawing of a landscape with hidden faces in the clouds, trees, etc. Witkin used geometric drawings with a simple figure, like a hexagon or a cube, hidden in a large complex figure. Other versions, especially for little children, may show a cat embedded in a maze of intertwined lines and other figures. The experimenter says, "Find the kitty. Touch the kitty."

Each of these three tests requires the individual to separate some item—his own body, a rod, or a drawing—from its background. Results suggest that field dependence, or independence, tends to be established early in life and to remain relatively stable.

Field independent people excel at problems where the different components have to be taken apart and reassembled. Socially, they are better able to resist group pressures than are the field dependent people, who tend to be more passive. In Witkin's experiment, more boys than girls were field independent.

The ability is partly due to constitutional characteristics and partly due to environment. Boys with overprotective mothers tended to be field dependent; boys whose mothers were not overprotective were more often field independent. (Might not this account for the difference in the showing of the sexes, since girls are commonly brought up in a more sheltered way?)

Another center of research on cognitive style is at the Menninger Foundation, an outgrowth of the famous Menninger Clinic in Topeka, Kansas. For some fifteen years, psychologist Riley Gardner and others, working within a framework drawn from several sources, including Piaget, have been seeking new ways to measure and identify dimensions of the mind.

The subjects who take their tests are volunteers paid for their time. They represent a wide range of occupations—college students, farmers, housewives, secretaries, teachers, etc. Church and fraternal groups sometimes come in a body, as a way of raising funds for their organizations. On at least one occasion, their test group was made up of twenty-eight pairs of husbands and wives, chosen partly as a way of getting people with the same social and economic background but also to get some information about comparative cognitive styles of married couples.

Just what is cognitive style? To illustrate, suppose you volunteer to take the Stroop Color Word Test. First you are handed a page of color names—red, green, blue, yellow—all printed in ordinary black and repeated over and over in varied order. You are asked to read it aloud as fast as you can, and your time is recorded. Next you are given a page of red, green, blue, and yellow asterisks and asked to call off the colors as fast as you can. Again your time is recorded.

Last—and here's the payoff—you are shown a page of those same four names printed in color, but it's always the wrong color. The word "red" might be printed in green ink, and so on. You are asked to call off the actual colors you see—never mind what the word says. How much are you slowed down by the conflict between the name you read and the color you see? If only a little, then your mind works in a flexible fashion and you will probably do well on intellectual tasks where there is stress or distraction. If a lot, then your style of thinking is more constricted and you are more interference prone.

It is interesting to note that one of Binet's early tests, when he was trying a variety of things and ten years before he developed his test for the Parisian school system, touched on this same point. First the subject read ten lines aloud and his time was recorded. Then he read ten similar lines while simultaneously writing the letters of the alphabet, and the two times were compared. Binet called this a test for "scope of attention" and did not include it in the famous Binet-Simon.

The Stroop Color Word Test, individually given, is not new, but at Menninger's they have developed a way of using it with groups by projecting the pages onto a screen, letting each person read silently and time himself by a large clock marked in seconds. The examiner cautions the assembled volunteers, "Your data will be of no help to us if you do not follow the instructions exactly." After showing a few practice lines on the screen, he says, "Now we will show you the page of words. Read the entire page as fast and accurately as you can, correcting all errors as you go. When you are finished with the page, record your reading time in seconds in the correct box and look up at me while sitting quietly so as not to distract any others who may still be reading. Ready. Watch the screen."

They do the same for the other two pages. On the last part, the page where the words and the colors conflict, the examiner says, "This part of the test is more difficult than Parts I and II. Try to remain still in spite of any

tendency you may feel to move in your chair. Please do
not sigh, laugh, or make any other audible sound."

The results of giving the test in this way to groups of
thirty or so at a time were reasonably valid and reliable
for experimental purposes and speeded up the collection
of data enormously.

Another dimension of the mind that influences
cognitive style concerns the way you spontaneously put
things into categories, working under free conditions. Do
you make few groups, or many? This seemingly trivial
trait has far-reaching implications and is measured by
the Gardner Object Sorting Test. You are given
seventy-three common objects—a bar of soap, a ham-
mer, and the like—and told to "Group the items in the
way that seems most logical, most natural and most
comfortable." When you have finished, you are asked
your reason for putting the things in each group.

The reasons can be anything. "They are all tools,"
"They are all in a kitchen," "All belong to a child," "All
have to do with smoking" are common examples given
for categories. But it is essential to the test that the
reason is asked for. Otherwise many people, after having
made some groups, put all the leftovers together into a
pseudo group not because of any similarity that they see
in them but just because they don't fit any of the other
categories. In such a "wastebasket" collection each item
is counted as a separate group.

Your score is the total number of categories you
arrange the objects into. The range is amazingly wide—
from as many as thirty to as few as three. The trait
proved to be remarkably stable and consistent. Whether
they are sorting household objects, pictures of people
cut out of magazines, or blocks with Chinese symbols on
them, some individuals just naturally divide things into
many small groups and other people make fewer groups
encompassing more items. The same thing held true for

a pencil-and-paper group test where fifty names of objects were to be sorted.

It isn't that people who make few groups lack the ability to see differences among objects, but they are more oriented to look for similarities. Others are more impressed by distinctions among things.

This raises some interesting questions for further research. One is that since learning new material often hinges on looking for similarities between the new and what you already know, might not this tendency to look for similarities have something to do with the ease with which new material is learned?

Another has to do with creativity. Writing in the *Bulletin of the Menninger Clinic, 1970*, Gardner said that, among children at least, those who arrange an assortment of heterogeneous objects into a few large groups are more explorative and more creative than those who sort the same objects into a number of small groups.

The whole thrust of the Menninger project is to identify different traits, each independent of the others but all contributing to individuality. For example, a person who is slowed down on the Color Word Test, is field dependent (Gardner and his associates accept Witkin's findings), and who makes a high score on the Object Sorting Test would have a very different learning style from one who has a different combination of highs and lows.

Another trait concerns the degree to which new experiences are infiltrated or colored by memories. It is measured by Gardner's Schematizing Test.

If you volunteer for this one, you are seated in a darkened room, and a square of white light is projected on the wall. You are given two seconds to look at it and six seconds to record your estimate of its size. Then other squares of white light are projected, one after another, and the same procedure is repeated each time. Unknown to you, the squares are getting bigger and bigger. How well can you keep up with the increases in size? Some people are pretty good at it. With others, the memory of the size the square was a few seconds ago mixes in with what they see now, and they lag behind, consistently estimating the square to be smaller than it actually is. This test, like a number of others, is plainly on perception.

When Piaget was guest lecturer at the Menninger School of Psychiatry for three weeks in March, 1961, it was perception that Gardner and his team of researchers wanted to discuss with him. Although Piaget is best known for his work on the way intelligence develops, he characterizes himself as an epistemologist—an investigator of the processes of human knowing. He has done experiments in many different areas, including perception.

He thinks that perception, being biased and subject to certain illusions, is inferior to the higher mental processes. Specifically, it is relative. For example, take a big chair and a little chair, identical except for size. If you look at them together, paying equal attention to each, the little one will appear smaller than it really is, the big one larger. That phrase "paying equal attention to each" is important. Piaget regards attention as the major link between perception and the higher mental operations.

A third body of experimental work on cognitive style is that of Harvard's Jerome Kagan and his colleagues. Kagan is one of the most outspoken critics of present IQ tests, which he considers seriously biased. In an article in the *Saturday Review*, December 4, 1971, he referred to "two similarly constructed standardized IQ tests invented by Caucasian middle-class Western men to rank-order everyone." He didn't call the tests by name but gave examples of six categories of questions from them—vocabulary, analogies, drawings with something missing, arithmetic, questions that ask the child what he would do in a given situation, and memory for strings of digits. (If you have read this book this far, you know what tests he is referring to.)

In his own experimental work, Kagan takes a different tack. He points out that problem-solving involves three distinct steps, in this order: First, the information is classified; second, it is stored in code form; third, it is transformed.

He feels that the importance of the first step has been underestimated in the past. Children presented with the same problem pay attention to different parts of it, then base their solution on the parts that caught their attention in the first place. (Note that this emphasis on attention fits what Piaget said on his visit to the Menninger Foundation about attention being the major link between perception and the higher mental operations.) They come out with different end results, not because of a difference in ability but because of a different way of choosing the initial information.

To find out more about this first step, Kagan used a Conceptual Style Test. He showed the child a card with three drawings of familiar objects on it—for example, a house with smoke coming out of the chimney, a book of matches, and a smoking pipe. He said, "Pick out two pictures that are alike or go together in some way."

The types of answers that children gave tended to fall into two groups, with clear differences between them. If the child said something like "The house and pipe both have smoke coming out," he was using an analytic style. If he said something like "The matches light the pipe," he was using a relational style.

Basically what the analytic child did was to mentally take the pictures apart and look for likenesses among the parts. If the card showed a watch, a man, and a ruler, he might say, "The watch and the ruler both have numbers." A child with a relational style of classifying information would be likely to say, "The man wears the watch," or, "The man uses the ruler."

In contrast to an IQ test, there are no right or wrong answers to the questions on Kagan's test. The objects can be paired in any way, and one style is no better than another. But the child's reasons reveal something important about his natural way of classifying and coding information. Kagan gave his test to 800 students in the elementary grades. He found that the relational answer was the most popular among little children and that the analytic style increased with age. For first-graders, the average was four analytic responses per student (out of thirty cards on the test). Sixth-graders averaged about ten analytic responses.

Research on cognitive style may also help to explain some still unsolved puzzles about conventional IQ tests. All teachers know children who consistently make high IQ scores but the only way you would know it is to go down to the principal's office and look up their records. Nothing in their performance indicates high ability.

Why don't they do as well as their tests indicate they should? If there are no apparent reasons—emotional disturbances or the like—the easy, all-purpose explanation is that they are lazy. Millions of words have been expended, rewards promised, and punishments meted out in an effort to get them to do better.

I don't think that it is always a case of laziness. Might not the fact that traditional tests are made up of fragments, coupled with the fact that the child may have an unusual cognitive style, produce misleading scores? I got the germ of this idea from a girl who seemed to fit that category. She said: "In those tests, the questions are all separate. Number two doesn't have anything to do with number one. I can do pages of those." But when it came to one long, organized task, she was no better than average.

When Galton first originated his mental tests, he said that he was "sinking shafts." This is what we're still doing in the present IQ tests. Then we take our collection of shallow core samples and, if they appear to show the same thing, we say, "Aha! There's an underlying stratum connecting them."

Maybe there is. But in the unknown and shifting terrain of the mind is this *always* true? How do we know that what we have tapped isn't a series of isolated pockets? And how about all the areas that present tests don't tap?

To sum up, IQ tests were oversold in the beginning and capabilities were attributed to them that they never had. For years they held undisputed sway in the schools— an article of faith second only to the Pledge of Allegiance. In the 1960's their power started to wane, and attention has turned to other approaches where, in some cases, experimentation has been quietly going on for a long time.

There are signs of possible convergences among views put forward quite separately by Piaget, Witkin, Gardner, Kagan, and others whose work I have not mentioned. It is possible that we may be near a breakthrough in the construction of new and better types of tests of mental ability.

*Bibliography*

BORING, EDWIN G., *A History of Experimental Psychology*, 2d ed. New York, Appleton-Century-Crofts, Inc., 1950.

———, *A History of Psychology in Autobiography*, Vol. IV. New York, Russell and Russell, 1968.

BRIM, ORVILLE G., CRUTCHFIELD, RICHARD S., AND HOLTZMAN, WAYNE H., *Intelligence: Perspectives 1965: The Terman-Otis Memorial Lectures*. New York, Harcourt, Brace & World, 1966.

BRIM, ORVILLE G., NEULINGER, JOHN, AND GLASS, DAVID C., *Experiences and Attitudes of American Adults Concerning Standardized Intelligence Tests*. New York, Russell Sage Foundation, 1965.

BUROS, OSCAR K., *The Mental Measurement Yearbooks*. Highland Park, New Jersey, Gryphon Press, 1941-65.

———, *Tests in Print*. Highland Park, New Jersey, Gryphon Press, 1961.

College Entrance Examination Board, *Bulletin of Information, 1971-1972*. Princeton, New Jersey, 1971.

———, *A Description of the College Board Scholastic Aptitude Test, 1971-1972*. Princeton, New Jersey, 1971.

151

— — —, *Report of the Commission on Tests, Righting the Balance*, Vol. I; *Briefs*, Vol. II. New York, 1970.

The Council for Exceptional Children, *State Laws Relating to the Evaluation of Exceptional Children.* Arlington, Virginia, 1971.

CRONBACH, LEE J., *Essentials of Psychological Testing*, 3d ed. New York, Harper & Row, 1970.

DARWIN, FRANCIS, *Rustic Sounds*, Chap. II. London, John Murray, 1917.

DENNIS, W., *Readings in the History of Psychology.* New York, Appleton-Century-Crofts, 1948.

FLAVELL, JOHN H., *The Developmental Psychology of Jean Piaget.* Princeton, New Jersey, Van Nostrand Co., 1963.

GALTON, FRANCIS, *Inquiries into Human Faculty and Its Development.* London, The Eugenics Society, 1883.

GARDNER, RILEY W., "Four Discussions with Professor Piaget." *Bulletin of the Menninger Clinic*, Vol. 26 (1962), pp. 117-19.

— — —, "Individuality in Development." *Bulletin of the Menninger Clinic*, Vol. 34 (1970), pp. 71-84.

GARDNER, RILEY W., AND LOHRENZ, LEANDER J., "Some Old and New Group Tests for the Study of Cognitive Controls and Intellectual Abilities." *Perceptual and Motor Skills*, Vol. 29 (1969), pp. 935-50.

GARDNER, RILEY W., LOHRENZ, LEANDER J., AND SCHOEN, ROBERT A., "Cognitive Control of Differentiation in the Perception of Persons and Objects." *Perceptual and Motor Skills*, Vol. 26 (1968), pp. 311-30.

GARDNER, RILEY W., AND SCHOEN, ROBERT A., "Differentiation and Abstraction in Concept Formation." *Psychological Monographs*, Vol. 76, No. 41 (1962).

GODDARD, HENRY H., "The Binet-Simon Measuring Scale for Intelligence." *The Training School*, January, 1910.

GOSLIN, DAVID A., *Criticism of Standardized Tests and Testing.* New York, Russell Sage Foundation, 1967.

HERRNSTEIN, RICHARD, AND BORING, EDWIN, *A Source Book in the History of Psychology*. Cambridge, Massachusetts, Harvard University Press, 1965.

HUNT, J. McV., *Intelligence and Experience*. New York, The Ronald Press Co., 1961.

INHELDER, BÄRBEL, AND PIAGET, JEAN, *The Growth of Logical Thinking from Childhood to Adolescence*. New York, Basic Books, 1958.

KAGAN, JEROME, ROSMAN, BERNICE L., DAY, DEBORAH, ALBERT, JOSEPH, AND PHILLIPS, WILLIAM, "Information Processing in the Child." *Psychological Monographs*, Vol. 78, No. 1 (1964).

LAURENDEAU, MONIQUE, AND PINARD, ADRIEN, *Casual Thinking in the Child*. New York, International Universities Press, 1962.

— — —, *The Development of the Concept of Space in the Child*. New York, International Universities Press, 1970.

LEE, LEE C., KAGAN, JEROME, AND RABSON, ALICE, "Influence of a Preference for Analytic Categorization upon Concept Acquisition." *Child Development*, Vol. 34 (1963), pp. 433-42.

MURCHISON, CARL, *A History of Psychology in Autobiography*, Vol. II. New York, Russell and Russell, 1961.

NUNNALLY, JUM C., *Introduction to Psychological Measurement*. New York, McGraw-Hill, 1970.

OTIS, ARTHUR S., AND LENNON, ROGER T., *Manual for Administration, Otis-Lennon Mental Ability Test*. New York, Harcourt, Brace & World, 1967.

PETERSON, J., *Early Conceptions and Tests of Intelligence*. New York, World Book Co., 1925.

PIAGET, JEAN, *The Child's Conception of Number*. New York, W. W. Norton, 1965.

— — —, *The Child's Conception of Physical Causality*. New York, Littlefield, 1965.

— — —, *Logic and Psychology*. New York, Basic Books, 1957.

PIAGET, JEAN, AND INHELDER, BÄRBEL, *The Child's Conception of Space*. New York, W. W. Norton, 1967.

— — —, *The Psychology of the Child*. New York, Basic Books, 1969.

PICHOT, PIERRE, "Alfred Binet," in *International Encyclopedia of the Social Sciences*. New York, Macmillan Co. and The Free Press, 1968.

PINARD, ADRIEN, AND LAURENDEAU, MONIQUE, "A Scale of Mental Development Based on the Theory of Piaget." *Journal of Research in Science Teaching*, Vol. 2 (1964), pp. 253-60.

POLLACK, ROBERT H., AND BRENNER, MARGARET J., *The Experimental Psychology of Alfred Binet*. New York, Springer, 1969.

TERMAN, LEWIS M., *The Measurement of Intelligence*. Boston, Houghton Mifflin, 1916.

TERMAN, LEWIS M., AND MERRILL, MAUD A., *Measuring Intelligence*. Boston, Houghton Mifflin, 1937.

— — —, *Stanford-Binet Intelligence Scale: Manual for the Third Revision Form L-M*. Boston, Houghton Mifflin, 1960.

VARON, EDITH J., "Alfred Binet's Concept of Intelligence." *Psychological Review*, Vol. 43 (1936), pp. 32-49.

WECHSLER, DAVID, *Wechsler Intelligence Scale for Children: Manual.* New York, The Psychological Corporation, 1949.

WITKIN, HERMAN A., "The Perception of the Upright." *Scientific American*, Vol. 200 (February, 1959), pp. 50-70.

WITKIN, HERMAN A., FATERSON, HANNA, GOODENOUGH, DONALD, AND BIRNBAUM, JUDITH, "Cognitive Patterning in Mildly Retarded Boys." *Child Development*, Vol. 37 (1966), pp. 301-16.

YERKES, R. M., "Psychological Examining in the United States Army." *Memoirs of the National Academy of Sciences*, Vol. 15 (1921).